Merl Reagle's
100th Anniversary
Crossword Book

Merl Reagle's
100th Anniversary
Crossword Book

For KAY WYNNE CUTLER

the youngest daughter of crossword inventor Arthur Wynne,
who graciously agreed to meet
and let us ask her a million questions

and

For MARIE HALEY

inventor of my career

Acknowledgments To:

Steve Kelley	Edward Frederick	Dennis Aramanda
Amy Lago	Mike Shenk	Lloyd Mazer

First Printing: November 2013   Second Printing: March 2014

Fourth Printing: November 2015

Copyright © 1980, 1985, 1990, 1991, 2002, 2003 2004, 2005, 2006, 2007, 2008, 2013, and 2014 by
    Merl H. Reagle

Published in the United States by The PuzzleWorks, P.O. Box 15066, Tampa FL 33684-5066

I.S.B.N. 978-0-9897825-0-0

Illustrations by Jim Borgman

Website: www.sundaycrosswords.com

4-Wd.

Normally, the Acknowledgments are on the other page, over there on the left, but as I began writing this foreword I started realizing that, with the 100th anniversary of the crossword puzzle upon us, I have more than the usual amount of acknowledging to do. And a lot to be thankful for.

This is the first crossword book of mine that my mother will never see. She died in January of this year. But if anyone is responsible for my being the way I am, it's her. I'm pretty sure I got my brains from her side of the family and my sense of humor from my dad's side — the best of both worlds. (The other way around would have made me a truck driver who can't tell a joke.) They were divorced when I was 10 and they hadn't seen or spoken to each other since 1962. Dad is still with us at 89 — born in 1924, the same year as the first crossword book, and he's still funny and sharp on the phone, despite a voice that gets a little raspier every year.

So first of all I want to thank them for giving me the puzzle gene and the sensibilities to do something constructive with it (no pun intended ... for a change).

Second, I must thank my better half, Marie, for making this preoccupation with puzzles an actual career. On my own I never would have flown all over the country going to feature editors' conventions and alternative newsweekly conventions and Sunday magazine editors' conventions to try to sell the crossword. It was Marie who said, "Come on, let's do it, let's go!" So we did, and one by one we kept getting papers — the San Francisco Examiner (later, the Chronicle), the Hartford Courant, the Seattle Times, the New York Observer, the Philadelphia Inquirer, the Cleveland Plain Dealer, the Los Angeles Times, the Arizona Daily Star, the Washington Post, and many others. This was Marie all the way, so thank you, sweetie. (And thank you, Izzy's Deli, formerly Kenny's Deli, in Santa Monica for being open 24 hours a day so that two earlybirds like us could meet.)

Third, a massive thank-you must go to Will Shortz, without whose friendship I would never have had such a rich and colorful career. Because of the American Crossword Puzzle Tournament, which Will founded, I have (1) met renowned crossword editor Margaret Farrar; not only met, but had lunch with her — twice — up in her New York apartment on 96th Street, (2) met crossword editor Will Weng and had lunch with him at the New York Athletic Club, (3) become part of a true crossword community that, before Will, had barely existed, if at all, and (4) met documentary filmmakers Patrick Creadon and Christine O'Malley and thus received the ultimate crossword trifecta — being in "Wordplay," which led to being on "Oprah!" and "The Simpsons."

And one more biggie — thank you, Arthur Wynne, for inventing this strange, addictive interlocking mind game called the crossword puzzle. The fact that it's all about things that cross and intersect makes it a great metaphor for people staying connected to each other. In Arthur's first eight years the crossword was still getting its sea legs, still a little wild, until Margaret standardized it in the 1920s and made it the multifaceted feature we know today. But it also seems appropriate that Arthur constructed the first crossword in the shape of a baseball diamond, evoking another American pastime. So, thank you, Margaret, for standing up to the plate and knocking the ball out of the park, but also, thank you, Arthur, for throwing that first pitch.

Merl Reagle

August 2013

My Guarantee — Twisted But Fair

The Father of the Crossword

There's a lot of information on the Internet about Arthur Wynne, and some of it is even true.

For example, it is true that he invented the crossword puzzle. Some people have disputed this, saying that puzzles involving crossing words had existed for many years before Wynne's creation, which is true. Wynne had solved many such puzzles himself as a boy in Liverpool, England, especially "word squares" similar to this one:

F O U R
O G R E
U R G E
R E E F

However, word squares are small and typically contain the same words across and down. In mid-December, 1913, Wynne's boss at the New York World wanted something more eye-catching for the Sunday-before-Christmas issue. With deadline approaching Wynne decided on a diamond-shaped grid with a hollowed-out center. The puzzle that was published on December 21, 1913, appears at right.

Arthur Wynne

Wynne would later say that he just synthesized a lot of ideas into one puzzle. For example:

• The grid was similar to others he'd seen, only bigger, containing 32 words instead of the usual eight or ten.

• It had numbers in the squares, perhaps Wynne's most distinctive innovation. Previous word puzzles either had no numbers in the squares or were made up of numbers alone, leaving the reader to draw the squares.

• Some rows contained multiple words (on either side of the diamond's hollow center). Ditto for the columns. Word squares had only one word in each row and column.

• All of the words were different, across and down.

Well, almost all of the words were different. Wynne's first effort did have a few peculiarities:
(1) The word DOVE appeared twice, the first time clued as "A bird" and the second time clued as "A

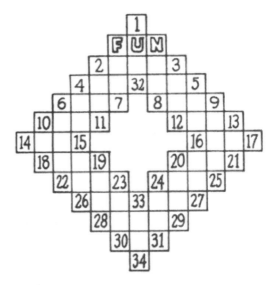

FUN'S Word-Cross Puzzle.

FILL in the small squares with words which agree with the following definitions:

2-3. What bargain hunters enjoy.
4-5. A written acknowledgement.
6-7. Such and nothing more.
10-11. A bird.
14-15. Opposed to less.
18-19. What this puzzle is.
22-23. An animal of prey.
26-27. The close of a day.
28-29. To elude.
30-31. The plural of is.
8-9. To cultivate.
12-13. A bar of wood or iron.
16-17. What artists learn to do.
20-21. Fastened.
24-25. Found on the seashore.

10-18. The fibre of the gomuti palm.
6-22. What we all should be.
4-26. A day dream.
2-11. A talon.
19-28. A pigeon.
F-7. Part of your head.
23-30. A river in Russia.
1-32. To govern.
33-34. An aromatic plant.
N-8. A fist.
24-31. To agree with.
3-12. Part of a ship.
20-29. One.
5-27. Exchanging.
9-25. Sunk in mud.
13-21. A boy.

pigeon." The fact that Wynne didn't notice it or didn't have time to change it has been something I've always chalked up to deadlines and the task of drawing the grid, which was new to everyone. (Today, a puzzlemaker's first urge would be to at least change one of the clues to something derivationally different, such as "the past tense of dive.")

(2) The numbers in the grid were written so large that there was no room to actually write letters in those squares — also a result of deadline pressure, I've always suspected. This was quickly changed in subsequent puzzles.

(3) For a puzzle with only 32 words, Wynne's first effort had quite a few, um, less-than-common entries, such as NEIF, SERE, TANE, NEVA,

and NARD, perhaps setting the stage for the common occurrence of such words in crosswords for years to come. Wynne's puzzle also contained the word DOH, which would be a snap to clue today — "Homer Simpson's exclamation" — but in 1913 Wynne had to go strictly by the dictionary and clue it as "the fibre of the gomuti palm." (D'oh! What else could it be?)

(4) Wynne's numbering system specified the first square *and* the last square of each answer. Thus, the clue "6-22" meant that the answer started in the "6" square and ended in the "22" square. This two-number cluing system existed for the entire eight years that Wynne was the puzzle editor and did not change until his successor deemed the second number unnecessary and dropped it.

His successor, by the way, was a young woman named Margaret Petherbridge, who today is credited not only with standardizing the crossword but helping to make it a publishing phenomenon. In 1924 she co-edited the first crossword book, which sold 400,000 copies in only a few months. It was a double first — the first-ever crossword puzzle book and the first book ever published by two tyros named Dick Simon and Max Schuster. Other volumes quickly followed, selling two million copies in just two years, and slingshotting Simon and Schuster into the publishing business. In 1926 Margaret left the New York World to get married, but she continued to edit the S&S books. In 1942, as Margaret P. Farrar, she became the first crossword editor of The New York Times.

According to Wynne's last wife, Dolly, Wynne's reaction to the runaway success of the crossword books in the mid-1920s was bittersweet. Back in 1914 Wynne had asked his bosses to patent or copyright the puzzle, but they had refused, calling it a passing fancy. So the only rights Wynne ever had were bragging rights; he said he "never made a penny" for having invented the country's most popular word puzzle. So no one was more surprised than Wynne that his young predecessor, Margaret, fresh out of Smith College, would be the engineer on the crossword express that was about to barrel across America.

But Wynne was resilient and resourceful. In addition to being a doting father he was three things at heart, a newspaperman, a violinist, and a puzzle fan. He continued to work at all three for the rest of his life. He worked for King Features, which was part of the Hearst organization, and he continued to make new and different types of puzzles into his 70s. He lived for many years in Cedar Grove, New Jersey, where he designed one of the town's churches. His face was one of the original caricatures on the wall of The Palm restaurant in New York City. Being a lover of music he played violin in various orchestras.

Despite being less than a household name even to most crossword fans, Arthur Wynne finally seems to be getting his due, thanks to the centennial year of his invention. I only wish he were here to see it. —MR

P.S. One of the main things that sets a true crossword puzzle apart from its ancestors is the black square. From January through September 1914, black squares did begin to appear in crosswords, but purely as chunky ornamentation. You could remove them and the puzzle would still be solvable, much like the first crossword with its hollow center — shading it black or leaving it white doesn't matter because there's enough white space there to separate the answers.

My question was, what was the first published crossword that had *utilitarian* black squares, that is, ones that were necessary to keep the words apart? Thanks to Brazilian puzzle archivist Sergio Barcellos Ximenes, I've pored through the first year of published crosswords and finally found a puzzle that absolutely required black squares where otherwise the answers would have run together.

And it's this hand-drawn pipsqueak that appeared on October 18, 1914. Remove the black squares and there's nothing separating the words near the center except for single white squares — and single white squares look like vacant squares to write in. So the black squares are utterly necessary. (If there's a puzzle earlier than this, let me know and I'll change it for the second edition!)

Finding Kay

About 15 years ago I found something on the Internet that started me on a quest. As you might guess, I am an incorrigible puzzlehead. I feel as if I have two brains, one that functions relatively normally (accent on "relatively") and one that is always looking for puzzle possibilities in every word, name, sentence, sign, headline, license plate, book title, show title, and movie title that I see. The relatively normal side may be only one-third of my entire noodle, but I am massively thankful that it's even that much.

I am also fascinated by the origins of things, especially how certain puzzles came to be — how they were created, who created them, where they first appeared, and so forth. During the 1980s I lived in Santa Monica, California, where surfing was something you did up the Pacific Coast Highway in Malibu, but after moving to Tampa, Florida, in the 1990s, surfing was something you did on this new thing called the Internet. And it was in 1998 that I found an obituary online that started me on a quest to uncover what to me was one of the great mysteries of puzzledom, a quest that involved Internet side trips to England and Brazil.

That 15-year quest ended today.

What I'd read online in 1998 was an old newspaper photostat of the obituary of Arthur Wynne, the inventor of the crossword. It was only a paragraph long, which to me was a shocking irony — a newspaper giving the ultimate short shrift to a man who invented something that appears in every newspaper. *In the world.* (Perhaps a double irony is that the newspaper that Wynne worked for when he invented the crossword was the New York World.)

But that much I knew. I knew that Arthur Wynne had grown up in Liverpool, England; that he had come to the U.S. when he was just 19, that he worked on a series of newspapers and played violin on the side, that he eventually became an editor at the New York World, that he created a diamond-shaped "word cross" puzzle that appeared in the paper on December 21, 1913 — the first crossword puzzle — that it became hugely popular, and that he died in 1945. This was all part of crossword lore that I'd known for many years.

What I did not know, and had never considered, was exactly where this amazing man had died. All these years I'd just assumed he'd died in New York or, at least, somewhere in New England. But in this obit, this puny paragraph, it said that Arthur Wynne, the inventor of the crossword, had died in Clearwater, Florida, twenty-five miles from the exact spot where, at that moment in 1998, I was reading the obit.

I was instantly filled with questions. Is he buried there? Are there any records? Would our local newspapers have anything in their archives? Are there any relatives I can talk to? Unfortunately, the Internet in 1998 was not what it is now. I came up empty at every turn.

And all the time I was searching I could't help thinking that Wynne's time in Florida might make an interesting local contest, maybe a puzzle treasure hunt in which Arthur Wynne's house or apartment would be the ultimate destination. For such a personage as Arthur Wynne to have a major connection to Tampa Bay, far away from the vaunted crossword corridors of New York City, seemed to be worthy of something more than just a brief news story or TV report. But again, it couldn't happen unless I could find some record of Wynne's last days.

And that's where things stood for several years, like a cold case file — always on my mind, but no new information.

Then in July 2012, I got a lead. I belong to an online puzzlemakers' site called Cruciverb, a subscription site anyone can join, but its purpose is to be a gathering place for crossword constructors, a place where newbies can ask questions of the pros, sort of a puzzlers' hangout. From time to time a tireless crossword researcher in Brazil named Sergio Barcellos Ximenes would drop a note to the list revealing his latest discoveries and providing links to them online. On July 31, 2012, he started posting information about Arthur Wynne, including one little factoid that seemed unimportant at the time, that Arthur Wynne had not only spent his last four years in Clearwater, 1941 to 1945, but that he was living with one of his daughters at the time. She was with him when he died at Morton Plant Hospital at age 74.

Flash forward to July 2013, one year later, and I'm in the process of preparing this book for publication, and it becomes all too clear to me that if there ever were a time to find out once and for all what happened to Arthur Wynne, it was now or never, the 100th anniversary of his invention. A friend of mine on the Tampa Bay Times (formerly the St. Petersburg Times) had searched the paper's voluminous archives, and even though the paper's obit was much longer, it still was lacking in new information. I decided to revisit the emails from Sergio and came up with another name, Vaast, the married name of Wynne's oldest daughter, Janet. This turned out to be the crucial clue.

But I wasn't the one who cracked the case. While I was out to lunch one day, my better half, Marie Haley, was doing some dogged Internet research of her own (I say dogged because I think she was a bloodhound in her former life). Marie was hot in pursuit of this oldest daughter, Janet, and what Marie found was initially deflating — Janet had died in 2007 — but in finding Janet, Marie had hit the mother lode, Janet's hometown obituary. It was extremely detailed, naming sons, daughters, husbands, wives and grandchildren, but the first relation mentioned was "a sister, Kay W. Cutler, 74, of Clearwater, Florida," and I just stood there, stunned. If this other sister, Kay, were still with us, she'd be 80 years old. Was she still in Clearwater? Is she the daughter that Arthur was living with when he died? If so, Kay would have been only 12 years old in 1945. The truth is, Arthur had remarried, to a woman who was 30+ years his junior, and he was not only "living with" his 12-year-old daughter, he and his wife were *raising her*. He'd become a father again at 62.

Marie and I had the same thought instantly — if Kay is actually right across the bay, *what's her phone number?*

It took Marie just five minutes to find it. And make the call. And a bright-sounding woman on the other end answered. The conversation lasted 15 minutes. We agreed to meet for breakfast at the Wildflower restaurant in Clearwater.

That day was today, August 1, 2013. And that's how we met and now know Arthur Wynne's youngest daughter, Kay. She walks with a cane but is still extremely sharp and laughs easily. She brought some articles about her father and has always wanted to set the record straight about his life.

She also led us to the site in Indian Rocks Beach where they lived, right on the gulf, with nothing but a short stretch of sand between their front door and the water. The apartment has changed a lot in 68 years, but it's still there. And I now know the address. The reason there was no funeral record or grave site is because he was cremated. Kay guesses that his ashes were probably scattered in the gulf, where he loved to fish.

We hope to have many more breakfasts and lunches with Kay. The stories she's told us about Arthur so far are utterly fascinating. We hope to be friends with her as long as we can. She has inspired us immeasurably.

That other meaning of August, the lowercase one that's pronounced au-*gust*, means "grand" or "awe-inspiring." Today was truly an august day.

Thank you, Marie. Thank you, Sergio. Thank you, Kay. And thank you, Arthur, for starting us on this journey. You have my eternal gratitude.

Merl Reagle
August 1, 2013

Kay Wynne Cutler and Merl Reagle

Sunday Puzzles

About the Puzzles

The first 42 crosswords in this book first appeared weekly in newspapers such as the Los Angeles Times, San Francisco Chronicle, Philadelphia Inquirer, and Washington Post between 2002 and 2008. All have been completely updated, re-edited, and reset in larger type exclusively for this edition.

To order extra copies of this book...

...please see the order forms on the last page, after the answers.

ACROSS

1 Mother of Hermes
5 Big tippler
9 1978 Sonia Braga role, Dona ___ (or backwards, to massage deeply)
13 National League home run champ of 2000
17 Long-running series
22 Source of "I have a little shadow …"
23 Steed need
24 Bible book
25 Author Rand
26 Store
27 King's genre
29 Juice-drink brand
31 Tiny tunneler
33 X's
43 Grifter's thing
46 Novel beginning?
47 Smack or switch ending
48 Inauguration highlight
49 Singer Carl Perkins was one
52 Tubular pasta
53 Desperate housewife Susan, really
54 Rose fruit
55 North Carolina university
56 Stuff in a closet
57 Tell's canton
58 Alley item
59 Car's front end?
61 Lothario's look
62 Student acquisitions
69 Topnotch
70 Bleeper in a blockbuster, 1977
71 Western Hemisphere org.
72 Thieves' outfoxer
73 Occupied, as the end of the bed
75 Stake in the game
76 Uncommon bills
78 Addict
79 Part of a balloon song
80 Classes that involve a lot of squeezing
84 Banjo man Scruggs
85 Pall of a sort
86 "The ___ see you …"
87 Siam visitor
88 Rapids, perhaps
92 Loser to DDE
93 ___ T
94 Of equal speed
99 Ice wish
102 Actor Gulager
104 Booth payment
107 Peruse
108 "The Red Wheelbarrow" poet
114 Airport technology
115 Place to plop
116 Britches breaches
117 Supreme leader?
118 "___ I say!"

DOWN

1 Very virile
2 Despise
3 More dangerous, as roads
4 Sharp tool
5 "Away ___!"
6 "___ joking!"
7 A conjunction
8 Rule: abbr.
9 Lifesaving Manhattan org.
10 "Crazy" bird
11 Not working
12 Modern Bible: abbr.
13 Type
14 Roughly speaking
15 Chowder cousin
16 Fool
18 "Go ahead, ___ ya!"
19 Mil. decoration
20 Grant's real name
21 Nuisances
22 Tree or remains
28 Lounge classic, "All ___"
29 Lend a hand
30 Slurpee cousin
31 Play opening?
32 Palindromic time
34 "Inside the NFL" regular
35 On
36 Pool circuits
37 Schedule anew, Variety-style
38 Bean and Welles
39 More slime-like
40 Primary motivation
41 Towel ending
42 Brat's target
43 He-Man's cartoon sister
44 Exaggerated work
45 Jackie's O
49 Ticket remainder
50 71 Across member
51 Old but new again
56 Staying power
58 Noted Quaker
59 The slim picture
60 ___ Paulo
61 Car-financing option
63 Hype
64 Ill-will
65 "Is that for here ___?" (restaurant query)
66 Air Force Academy freshman
67 Actress Verdugo
68 Dear ones?
73 Cooking fat
74 On ___ with
75 Summits
76 Said thrice, a film
77 PBS's flagship station in NYC
78 JFK was in it
80 Tennis great
81 A solvent, familiarly
82 Capt. Kirk's home state
83 Lip
89 Home of the Governator: abbr.
90 180° maneuver
91 Wimbledon exchange
95 ___-Lay
96 Circe's all-vowel island
97 Actress Emma of "Dynasty"
98 QB successes
99 Copter forerunner
100 Patron saint of Norway
101 Car's front end?
102 USSR, to a Russian
103 Asian nation
104 General ___ Chicken
105 Night predators
106 Fleur-de-___
108 Mg. and kg., e.g.
109 Word with base or ball
110 Sprint rival
111 Stamped item: abbr.
112 Gaucho gold
113 Notorious psychedelic

ACROSS

1 Tied (up)
8 Frat candidate
14 Sitting Bull was one
20 Ventilation source
21 "The Bathers" painter
22 Magic potion
23 Indie theater locale
25 1950s-80s TV actor, Harold ___
26 Look hard
27 ___ facto
28 "I'll have the ___"
29 It helps you get a clear picture
38 With 8 Down, a type of alcohol
41 Wiener schnitzel meat
42 Capital on the Mediterranean
43 Com preceder
44 Slangy sailor
45 Nonexistent
46 Prior to, old-style
48 Casino order
50 Shout in a kids' game
56 Mushroom heads
57 Speaking style
58 Took steps
59 Ideal guy
61 Pola of the silents
62 Praise highly
63 Subarctic forest
65 Tom Jones hit
72 Much-in-demand
73 Stadium accesses
74 "And that's ___!"
75 Sweet-looking
79 Photo finish?
80 "___ Kick Out of You"
81 Terrible
82 It has the same melody as "The Alphabet Song" and "Twinkle, Twinkle, Little Star"
87 Priest's urging
89 Like teardrops
90 "Told ya so!"
91 Election and leap, for ex.
92 Big-leaguer
93 Zipper alternative
96 Arthur of "Shane"
98 Kin of -speak
99 Nursery rhyme start
105 Shady giants
106 Some sisters
107 Site of a 1967 war
111 E to E, e.g.
114 Styne, Comden, and Green song from their hit 1954 musical
119 Wonderland service
120 Disinclined
121 Like some dyes
122 Lay ___ (resolve)
123 See 109 Down
124 Basic spans, in music

DOWN

1 New Mexico art colony
2 Breach
3 City in SE Turkey
4 Low on cash
5 The RAF, in a Churchill quote
6 North Pole hiree
7 Ball belle, briefly
8 See 38 Across
9 Most picayune
10 Fund, as a museum
11 Stock index pioneer
12 Actress Scala of "The Guns of Navarone"
13 Arch extension
14 Real-life rerun
15 1920s New York governor known as "the Happy Warrior"
16 High-flying toys
17 Losing tic-tac-toe line
18 Its symbol is Sn
19 A word with you?
24 Working girl in a Beatles song
28 Jordan neighbor: abbr.
30 Bad to the bone
31 "Little" Dickens girl
32 Saver's buy during WWII
33 Spongy ball brand
34 Arena level
35 Luggage attachment
36 Pizazz
37 Atomic event, in headlines
38 "How fast was ___, officer?"
39 Fuse, in a way
40 Accommodate
45 Very small
46 Songwriter Hoyt
47 Have no ailments whatsoever, maybe
49 Here, over there
51 Knight time?
52 Main vertical lines on graphs
53 Eightsome
54 Where Meridian is, in gazetteer shorthand
55 Therefore
60 Tawdry
62 Novelist Jong
63 Certain Sri Lankan
64 Watchdog grp.?
66 Slick-talking
67 Passed fast
68 Weather stat
69 Cyclops feature
70 British moms
71 Slip away, as time
75 Adjust
76 Part of TNT
77 Horse handler
78 Velvet add-on
79 Lively dance
83 Novelist Sholem
84 Uncovered
85 Kin of Edw., Jos., and Thos.
86 Dorothy and Toto's st.
88 Changes gradually
94 Kelly the clown
95 USN officers
96 Olympian Bruce
97 Highlands dialect
100 Poke fun at
101 Motionless
102 Derby prize
103 Court fop in "Hamlet"
104 Nabisco's ___ Wafers
108 It gets hammered
109 She's Eve in "All About Eve"
110 Date to beware
111 Superstar of the Polo Grounds
112 Head cheese?
113 Slangy sailor
114 Catch
115 Stowe girl
116 Irritate
117 Cleaning appliance, briefly
118 USN officer

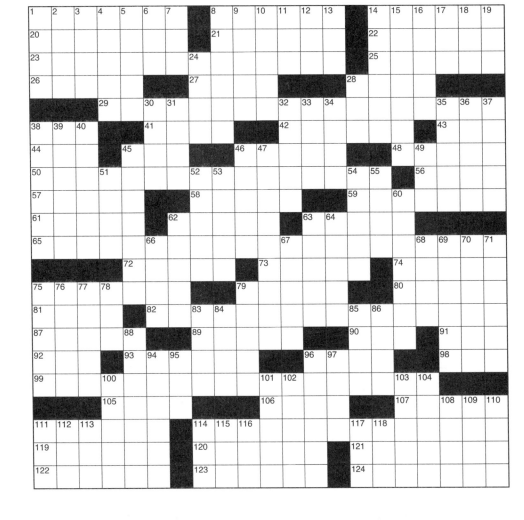

3 | Snacks on a Plane

…Less painful than snakes, and they taste better

ACROSS

1 Knit suit designer (and a Nancy Reagan fave)
7 Sweat it
11 Cruise-taker's woe
19 "That's that"
20 Philosophy
21 Unreal
22 Snack capital of America?
24 Catches off guard
25 Soviet space program
26 Slop-lover's comments
27 Sport spot
28 Exist extension
29 Curly coif
31 Snack-loving news analyst?
34 Clay, today
37 "Ed Wood" star
39 Henrik's Mrs. Helmer
40 Abductor of P.H.
41 Mr. Magritte
43 From Oslo's country, to a native
46 Devine and Flanders
48 German coal city
52 Snack-lover's favorite drink?
55 Walmart founder's name
57 Charles Lamb's pseudonym
58 Extras
59 Sugar shape
60 Tuneful tearjerker
62 Hr. fractions
63 Mortise mates
65 ___ Traffic Keep Left
66 Horror maven Craven
67 Spike Lee's snack admission?
71 The Falcons, briefly
73 Given the boot
74 Actor Hamilton of "Jaws" and "The Graduate"
75 Flood survivor
77 1 of 3
79 Be the end of
80 Founder of the Shakers
82 Series opener?
83 Gruesome-graphics show
85 Snack-loving dessert maker?
87 Refine, as copper
89 Placed inside, as a pkg.
91 Keel scraper
92 River zappers
93 Wonderment
95 Swedish import
97 Eye part
99 QU filler
100 Snack-lovin' athlete's error?
106 Old petroleum co.
108 "___ momento"
109 Disdain
110 Actress Watts
112 Piece of land
116 Dinky drink, to an innkeeper
118 Preparin' to eat some granola, snack-style?
120 Giggled
121 Auxiliary building
122 "Eeeek!"
123 Ticket riskers
124 Fannie, Ginnie, and Sallie
125 Pump levy

DOWN

1 Lethal injectors?
2 Nabisco brand, Stella ___
3 Don't ignore, as signs
4 Abatement
5 Effervesced
6 Rodeo Hall of Famer Berry (whose name sounds like a grain)
7 Old French bread?
8 Officer Andy of "Hill Street Blues"
9 Cofounder of GE
10 ___ degree
11 Interprets incorrectly
12 Modify
13 Colombian plains
14 Sturdy
15 Founded: abbr.
16 Distance runner
17 Surprise party, e.g.
18 Takes a break
20 XX% of DXXX
23 City near Vandenberg AFB
27 Yorkshire river
30 Doesn't own, perhaps
32 Hawaiian coffee
33 Lessens
34 Angel's instrument, in Rome
35 City on the 27 Down
36 Sagging, as sales
38 Carry on
42 Cain's eldest
44 Thrown, as over the shoulder
45 Explosion sound
47 Walk nonchalantly
49 Drawler, perhaps
50 Mozart's "a"
51 Badgers
53 Open, in a way
54 ___ adhesive
56 Sportscaster Albert
61 Spanish chaperon
63 Jungle menace
64 Biplane supports
65 "It's later ___ think"
68 One with a reserved parking space
69 Grade school subj.
70 "The Little Girl ___ Knew"
71 Dough machines
72 Little off the top
76 Gala wear, maybe
78 Rice ___
80 Van Gogh's city
81 While opening
84 Ripped to pieces
85 Give away, as a secret
86 Mine mess
88 Distorted
90 Normandy city
94 Audience shout
96 Cream pie ingredient
98 Attack ailment
100 Necessities
101 Nerdy, perhaps
102 "Tender Mercies" penner Horton
103 Copier refill
104 "Rawhide" singer
105 Takes a drubbing
107 Snacks for Santa
111 Trail ___
113 Border on
114 Hermosillo home
115 Oft-animated monster, briefly
117 Rd. with a no.
118 Zodiac animal
119 It's game?

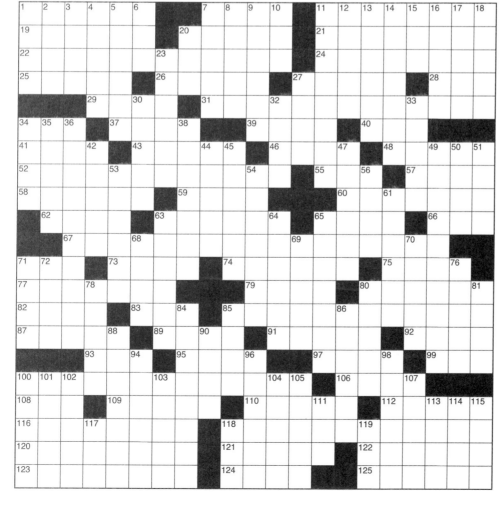

NOTE: *English has a lot of "idiomatic married couples." For example, a woman with very little on is rarely described as barely clad or minimally clad, but always "scantily clad." How these two words got "married" I'm not sure, but here's a sampling. (If "scantily clad" were an answer, it would be clued, "Not just minimally c---, but ___ c---." The letter with hyphens hints at the word "clad.")*

ACROSS

1 It comes after E.
5 "Kudzu" cartoonist Marlette
9 Starting
13 Web site help, briefly
17 Not just very c----, but ___ c----
21 Border (on)
22 Not just the plain t----, but the ___ t----
23 Wall St. index: abbr.
24 Mr. Barnum
25 T or F, on exams
26 Bass ___
28 TV Tarzan Ron
29 Hans, in Ireland
30 Abbr. after a Bismarck politico's name
31 Work the land
33 Passbook nos.
35 Have one's fill

36 Not just a great i---, but a ___ i---
40 Decompose
41 *Quattro* minus *uno*
42 Simba or Nala
43 In the style of
44 Skillet
47 Not just w--- well, but w--- ___
52 Praising work
53 Do a flour job
54 River lurker
55 Lechers
56 "I do," for one
57 Pluto et al.
58 "Kinsey" star's first name
61 Fab opening
62 Transmitted
63 Another helping
64 Not just a total a------, but a ___ a------
68 Hall of Famer Speaker
69 Yemen's chief port
70 Skeleton starter
71 Actor Andrews
72 Comes down with
73 Fisherman's name?
74 World book?
76 Hardly friendly
78 Get in the game
79 It climbs the walls
80 Not just at high s----, but at ___ s----
84 Sans anxiety

86 Dawn goddess
87 Land unit
88 Buddy
91 ___ Dhabi
92 Not just a large s--, but a ___ s--
96 Tact add-on
97 Newsroom measures
99 Top-notch
100 Singer Bobby
101 Boot bottom
102 Fluid in a well
103 Circle overhead?
105 Longing
106 Hero, perhaps
109 Place for polish
111 Not just g-- ----- well, but g-- ----- ___
115 Fan mag, to fans
116 Not just very d-----, but ___ d-----
117 Jason's vessel
118 Body opening?
119 José's half-dozen
120 Is worth the effort

DOWN

1 Beach Boys hit, "I ___ Music"
2 Render unnecessary
3 Strip about a blonde teen
4 Memo opener
5 Speaker's spot
6 Clip-___

7 1960s U.N. chief
8 Actress Jackson
9 It might be courageous
10 35mm camera, initially
11 Body of work
12 Bluebeard's last wife
13 Fleeting fashion
14 Not just terrible p------, but ___ p------
15 Winter warmer
16 Doesn't go
18 Big molecule
19 QB's pickup
20 Greek letter
22 Truman's win, e.g.
27 King of TV et al.
30 Dentist's request
31 You can get caught on it
32 Oil-well firefighter Red
34 Evasive
36 Staff symbols
37 "___ that just too bad"
38 Poker pile
39 On the ___ (at large)
44 On-the-39 Down type
45 Poster boy
46 Capek's "War with the ___"
47 Add lanes to
48 Lennon Sisters discoverer
49 Greek masterwork
50 "Sorry"
51 Wise advisor
53 Not just particularly l------, but ___ l------
57 Chocolate giant
59 "I/Rock" insert
60 Frenzied
62 Place
63 Mysteriously wonderful
64 Second attempt
65 Under-car bar
66 Hurricane-monitoring agcy.
67 Approach
72 Crest rival
74 Red from embarrassment
75 Coil of yarn
77 Belgian violinist Eugene
78 -vian preceder
81 Zilch
82 Laptop key
83 Some laptops
85 Wharton deg.
88 With reverence
89 Gene forms
90 Suspicious
92 Daughter of Picasso
93 Rummage through
94 Happenings
95 "A Wrinkle in Time" author Madeleine
97 "South Pacific" Tony winner
98 "... bombs bursting ___"
101 Take a dive, perhaps
104 Add years to one's life
105 Not hither
106 X-ray units
107 Comic Philips
108 Dial or Tone, e.g.
110 Gene in "The Producers"
112 Army member?
113 Island keepsake
114 Memo opener

5 George Steinbrenner for President
...*Playing politics*

ACROSS

1 The slammer
5 End of a Smith Barney slogan
11 Turf by the surf
16 Like the views of George's opponent?
19 Donald, to Dewey
20 Presidential campaigns, to George?
21 Cop crony of D.A. Burger
24 As written
25 *Océan* content
26 Deserter
27 Troll kin
28 Mag cover abbr.
29 Jolt
31 Herbal beverage
33 Biblical twin
36 "What ___ be alive!"
38 Sauce staple
40 Quick campaign appearance by George?
44 Greek letters
45 "___ man with seven wives ..."
46 God for whom a day of the week is named
47 Criticizes
48 Cheat sheets
49 Heavy fruit
51 Baseball's Mel
52 "___ Fideles"
54 Scottish river or firth
55 Like his opponent's tactics, according to George?
58 Actress Jane
60 Mark (down)
63 Course for new arrivals: abbr.
64 You, in your head
65 Legal authority?: abbr.
67 Took off
69 Greenhouse louse
71 George's word for his opponent?
75 Asian goat antelope
76 Puzzling bird
77 Chick follower
78 It can be aroused
79 Toward the tail
81 Smash sign
82 "Honest!"
84 Campaigning desperately, like George's opponent?
89 A dir.
90 Half an ice cream flavor
92 Arts org.
93 "Get down"
97 "___ easy as 1-2-3"
99 Math branch
100 Rural lass
101 Hat or race
102 Lady's address
103 Stay in contact, George-style?
105 Calm
106 One way to be paid
108 Defense org.
109 Buddy and Rob's TV pal
111 Geo. and Jude, e.g.
112 Puncture starter
113 Quick preview
115 Dash meas.
118 "Losing My Religion" group
120 Machine part
122 More dweeblike
124 What George's opponent did?
128 Swedish import
129 How George views the China issue?
130 Adlai's 1956 running mate
131 Down ducks
132 English school

DOWN

1 Controversial billboard character
2 U.N. VIP
3 "Would ___?"
4 Smooth, in music
5 Summer in the *cité*
6 A distance
7 Baltic port
8 Asexual
9 Project add-on
10 Sun. scores
11 Black Sea country: abbr.
12 Draw into self-incrimination
13 Behaved
14 Transparent: abbr.
15 George's political friends?
16 Dix and Knox: abbr.
17 Rootlike stem
18 Chimney feature
22 Support, as George?
23 8 by 10 ___
27 Beat at biking
30 French designer Jean
32 American Fur Co. founder, 1808
34 Valued violin
35 Muttered mot
37 Sheet music abbr.
38 Baseball's McCarver
39 Fresh from Hawaii
41 Not yon
42 Powerless condition?
43 CIA antecedent
48 Baseball's Ron
50 Radical '60s org.
53 Old airline
56 Other than us
57 Hopeless
59 Brown drink
60 Malfunction, as a rifle
61 Liberal platform of George's opponent?
62 Tries to trick George during a debate?
66 Ho-hum
68 Date minimum
70 Ailing
72 Spare-tire place
73 "And ___ friend" (host's request)
74 Vergil subject
75 Took long steps
77 Part of i.p.s.
80 Tide rival
83 Contingent factors
85 New York city
86 When bats fly
87 Blasts (of laughter)
88 Industrious ones
89 Apelike
91 ___-Aztecan (language group)
94 Actress Wyler or singer Wilson
95 Arabia's founder
96 Storm center
98 Doc bloc: abbr.
103 "___ of St. Agnes" (Keats)
104 1975 film, "A ___ His Dog"
105 Untwisted silk (not a shirt part)
107 Splashed down?
110 Forms bands of sparks
114 Enamoring god
116 Dick Van ___
117 Futures dealer?
119 ___ Helens
121 Pvt. investigators?
123 68 Down, in Guaymas
124 Joe-___ weed
125 My ___, Vietnam
126 Plaines starter
127 Magnon starter

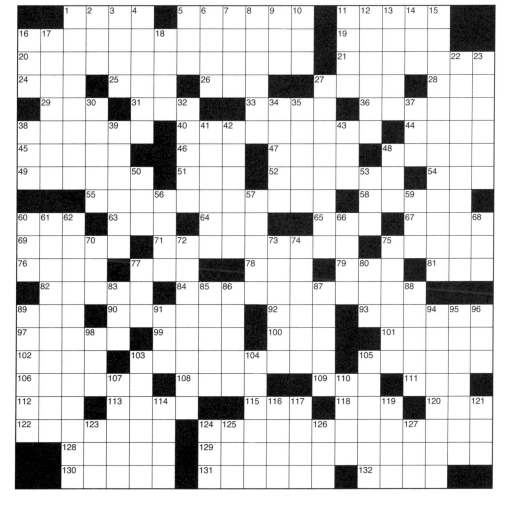

Triple Doubles

...I've got three pair. What have you got?

ACROSS

1 Nadir
7 Bygone mail abbr.
10 Copyright relatives: abbr.
13 Letter from Greece?
16 Big name in skin care products
17 One of the 12 spies of Moses
19 Recruit's place
21 800 number, e.g.
23 Doesn't object to
24 1968 O.C. Smith hit
26 Actress Ryan
29 Iranian coin
30 Learning ctr.
31 Hurry, old-style
32 Huts and flats
34 Last Tudor monarch
40 Took a cable car
41 City on the Ruhr
44 Big name in home security
45 "Rubber Ball" singer
46 Super-bright movie set equipment, ___ lights
48 "Bodily" follower
49 Clashers in the studio, maybe
52 It makes waves
54 ABC show since 2003
57 Cozy retreats
58 Board game turn
59 Bern's river
60 Total disaster
62 Soak (up)
65 Indulge oneself on a day off
70 Above, to a bard
71 Dry gulch
73 Wreck
74 Mechanization prefix
76 Editor's override
77 Often glossy volume
84 Tests the weight of
86 Cartoonist Syd
87 Mongolian desert
88 Shah Jahan's city
89 Casino owners' org.
90 Part of an island welcome
92 She played Anna in "Anna Christie"
94 Tippi's "Marnie" co-star
95 Quitting-time shout, on TV
101 "Word is ..."
103 Former ringmaster?
104 Old character
105 Kin of "yikes!"
107 PBS benefactor
108 With 115 Across, a 1955 comedy
114 Very long time
115 See 108 Across
119 Chew out
120 Composer Morricone
121 Parlor piece
122 Flat-faced flyer
123 It ends in Nov.
124 The Blue Jays, on scoreboards
125 Ballpark section

DOWN

1 Cave dweller
2 Lacto-___-vegetarian
3 Bus. card abbr.
4 Ace archer
5 Burning
6 Recess for a joint
7 Rev at high speed
8 Patriotic lapel pin
9 Actress Dolores
10 Roman cover-up?
11 Changed, sci-fi-style
12 Enter, in a way
13 Zap, in a way
14 "Famous" cookie man
15 Buffy's old network
17 Purse phone
18 Hit a mixer button
19 Language group that includes Zulu
20 Tabloid target
22 Airport info, briefly
25 Atty.'s title
26 Head of the Secret Service, 2006-13, ___ Sullivan
27 Carlo Levi's "Christ Stopped at ___"
28 Fade
33 Judges
34 Birth of a notion?
35 Free, in a way
36 Little or no effort
37 Nevertheless
38 Telecommunication?
39 Motion detector
42 Excel
43 "The End of Faith" author Harris
47 "Let Me Entertain You" musical
49 Its HQ is in Lod, Israel
50 Scout type
51 Pizzeria need
53 Tenet's former org.
55 About 2.2 lbs.
56 "Mule Train" singer
60 Put one over on
61 Sacked out
62 Strut one's stuff
63 Popular salsa brand
64 Ready-made home
66 Smack or switch ending
67 Bit of smoke
68 Bit of bickering
69 Move like Uranus
72 Giants manager before Durocher
75 Way too weighty
77 ___ Pet
78 Frozen-waffle brand
79 Santiago charger?
80 Face on a fiver
81 City near Buffalo
82 Windy City hub
83 Rather, informally
85 Zigzagged downhill
91 Sentence reducers?
93 Lacking purpose
96 Tower city
97 Small goose
98 Frank holder
99 "You ___ both"
100 Presentable
102 Bean cover?
105 A Ringling brother
106 Half a laugh
108 Keep ___ profile
109 79 Down, in San Diego
110 Perfectly
111 With -phile, a wine lover
112 Recipe direction
113 Go ___ winner
114 Presidential monogram
116 Pt. of a chain
117 Avg. size
118 Triumphant cry

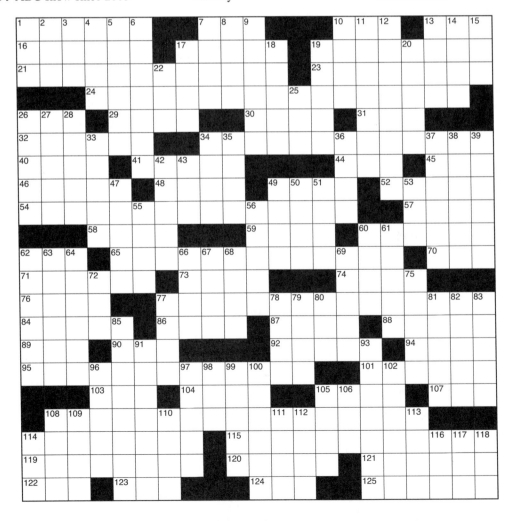

ACROSS

1 Lesser leagues
7 Scopes Trial org.
11 Scoff
15 Eggs
18 Astronomy Muse
19 Without letup
21 Bar between Pirellis
22 Hitchcock's title
23 "___ ... I'll be with you in just a sec ..."
25 Powerful
27 Was positive about
28 Place for a pad
29 Oil-exporting emirate
31 Bullet-train city
32 Mesopotamia, today
34 "So ... I heard that you stopped seeing that ___ ..."
36 Backspace over text
39 Let go, in a way
42 Undoing word
43 "Good for you! He was ___ ..."
45 TV oldie about Johnny Yuma
50 Home of the 20s?
51 Record the price of again
52 Nureyev's company, once
54 City on the Truckee
55 Applications
57 View from Long Isl.
58 Finished an operation
60 Joke
61 Scoundrels
63 "... Consider yourself lucky. My last boyfriend was a regular ___ ..."
66 Crow relative?
68 Sum anew
69 Doesn't feel so hot
70 "So ... how would you like ___?"
73 Sun streams
75 Spigoted server
76 Justice appointed by Ford
77 Satisfied sounds
78 Phony nickel
82 Bowie's "___ Dance"
84 Dodger great
85 Widen
88 Start of "Love Letters"
89 "Married ... with Children" star
91 "Should I square it off in the back or do you want it ___?"
93 Big ___ house
94 Flies around Africa
96 Amo
97 "Okay, and I'll finish up with ___ ..."
102 Pacific cruise sighting
104 Actress Judi
105 Had in mind
106 Italian beach resort
108 Collections
112 Worked the Dial
114 "Oh, by the way ... did you hear about ... where was I? ... and another thing ..."
117 Common contraction
118 Ripped
119 Be miserly
120 "A Browser's Dictionary" author John
121 ___ canto
122 "Orinoco Flow" singer
123 Mr. Ferrari
124 Mariel's granddad

DOWN

1 Pond mud
2 Essential mineral
3 Specify
4 Cheap genie's offer
5 Tuneful city "by the sea-o"
6 Drink once pitched by Robert Young
7 Frank or Seymour
8 Dots and dashes, e.g.
9 Stonewall Jackson's C.O.
10 Lopsided
11 Baseball-loving country
12 Affluent area outside a city
13 First name in pharmaceuticals
14 "No ___ the wicked"
15 See 31 Across
16 LPs and 45s
17 Holder of Leia's secret
20 Sturdy carts
24 Coroners' probes
26 More satiny
30 Q follower
33 Parking place, often
34 Secluded valley
35 Lopsided
36 Biblical twin
37 Well-worn ways
38 Zenith
40 Form of salt?
41 Southern org.
44 Tread loss, e.g.
45 "Yours" follower
46 Israeli folk dance
47 British actress Reid
48 Author Bagnold and actress Markey
49 Ear feature
52 TV puppet
53 Po land?
56 Badge of battle
58 Lots
59 June observance
62 Disgusted comments
63 Ballet leaps
64 Make up (for)
65 Boo companion
66 Drilled
67 Reach a cost of
68 Loud party
70 Present time?
71 Of a heart part
72 Highland dance
73 Liszt effort
74 ___ Spumante
77 They enable a fly to fly
79 Gray wolf
80 Rice, for one: abbr.
81 Boarding place
83 Abduct
85 Lavish attention (on)
86 Possessive pronoun
87 Word maven Partridge
90 Art lover
91 With a will
92 Point Barrow resident
94 ___ certain extent
95 Some DVD players
97 Wing it
98 Get along
99 Big name in chips
100 Abrasive substance
101 Jason's wife
103 Rolls partner
106 Film actress Kay (who has an apt-sounding last name)
107 Hand ___ (congratulate)
109 Brönte orphan
110 Small amounts
111 Burlesque or Burnett bit
113 Secretariat rider Turcotte
115 Reunion attendees
116 Clothes dryer?

ACROSS

1 Frighten
6 Twenty containers
10 "___ la vie"
14 Hellion's forte
16 Accepted principle
18 Start running seriously
21 Director Jean-___ Godard
22 Dough for noodles
23 Visit
24 Island paste
25 Sober
27 Actress Sommer
29 Shock
31 Mrs. Helmsley
33 Possibly will
34 Word heard in "Sloop John B"
37 Noninterference
41 Women's ___
42 Jury members
44 Food or music preceder
45 Game requiring three walls
49 Target of a practical joke
52 Repetitive composition
56 When Juliet drinks the potion
57 Fed. property manager
59 Bossy girl?
62 Word of acceptance
63 "Was ___ harsh?"
65 Capital of Sicily
68 Imitated
69 John Singer Sargent was one
72 Per item
75 Brings into harmony
76 Appear dramatically
77 Bush whacker?
80 Regular post
82 Set shout
83 Florida's ___ AFB
85 Cellist Casals
86 Actor Herrmann
90 Attack from above
92 India and invisible
95 "___ clichés like the plague"
97 Shakespearean exclamation
98 Asian capital
103 Underage teen, in street slang
108 "Big Blue"
109 Honda rival
110 Venomous hisser
111 Actress Lanchester
112 Practice 37 Across
115 H2O, for one: abbr.
116 Scourge of 1918
118 "A clue!"
121 Deli order
122 Bobby Vinton hit of 1963
127 Headline-making Cuban boy
128 Walmart, e.g.
129 Blue hue
130 Wineglass part
131 Broken piece

DOWN

1 Waited, perhaps
2 San Francisco, e.g.
3 Late tennis great
4 1840 Wagner opera about an Italian patriot
5 Placed inside: abbr.
6 Pinnacle
7 It's on a roll
8 Farrow or Hamm
9 Takes potshots
10 Friendly waggers
11 Office ph. line
12 Letter opener
13 Perfectly
14 Lake of "Hairspray"
15 Circus reaction
17 Home of Little Havana
18 Island dance
19 Messy substances
20 Story teller
21 NASA moon lander
26 Coloring stuff
28 Chou ___
30 Snowy peak
31 Shopper's compilation
32 Type of 26 Down
35 Italy's Berlusconi
36 Lawyers' org.
37 Island memento
38 Trajectory, e.g.
39 Fierceness
40 Baseball's Roberto or Sandy
43 "Green Acres" first name
45 The great Gatsby
46 Score 100% on
47 "___ open!"
48 "Sorry, ___ run"
50 Concept
51 Henner of "Taxi"
53 Little rest
54 Game of Clue need
55 Screwy
58 See 90 Across
60 "Well, ___ crook" (Nixon)
61 ___-Rooter
64 Coal carrier
65 Wrestler's goal
66 Had something
67 Collectible platters
69 Composer Glass
70 "___ Lang Syne"
71 "Kick it up a notch!" chef
72 Precognition, e.g.
73 ___ for effort
74 Part of a pickup
77 In the style of
78 Noon on some clocks
79 The last word?
81 Solitary
82 Start of the fifth century
84 Diving bird
87 Thirsty tot's request
88 Lana contemporary
89 "Cocoon" director's first name
91 "___ knew then ..."
93 Hunter who played Stella
94 Endurance
96 Some CD players
98 "Open ___ 9"
99 Assist, in a way
100 Melissa Etheridge hit, "___ Only One"
101 Sea fed by the Don
102 Time wasters
104 Poitier film, "___ of Blue"
105 Bold poker bet
106 "The Heat ___"
107 Invoice add-on
110 Saab competitor
113 Banjo virtuoso Fleck
114 Actor La Salle
116 Destiny
117 Portrayer of Oskar (Schindler)
119 Gag reflex?
120 Seaweed product
123 *Evian, par exemple*
124 Predetermined
125 They, in Calais
126 First ___

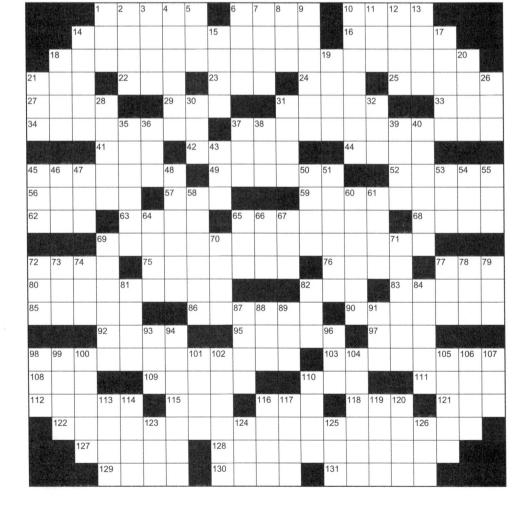

Dog Breeds I'd Like To See

...Time to bone up again

ACROSS

1 Year No. 2 of the 12th century
5 Mystique
9 Fails to pass
15 John Wayne cop film of 1974
18 Popular golf course dog?
21 Sigma follower
22 Dog so cute you could eat him up?
24 Protest of a sort
25 Pop quiz, e.g.
26 Impulses
27 FDR project
30 How this ans. runs
31 Watched warily
33 Ye ___ Pie Shoppe
34 Annoyingly smart dog?
39 With distinct breaks betw. successive tones
43 Wild about
44 Pizazz
45 Big name in talk
48 Writer LeShan
49 Sleep-loving dog?
53 Frisbee-catching dog?
56 Green need
57 Hosp. scan
58 Leaf pore
60 Mortal enemy
61 Second introduction?
63 Lifts with effort
65 Great-sounding Horne
66 Dog that says "bark" instead of actually barking?
71 Dog that can chew his way through a wall?
75 Erstwhile "Tonight" show host
76 Crusoe's creator
78 Cannes milk
79 Implants deeply
83 Chick at the piano
85 Word after "Monsters" or "Murder"
86 ___ degree
89 Dog with a purple tongue?
91 Dog that likes old-fashioned dance music?
94 Notable time
95 Verdun's river
96 Hunky-dory
97 Answer to a judge
98 Knocks
100 Dog that never stops eating?
106 "___-daisy!"
109 Managed-care choices
110 Complaint you "pick"
111 "Only this, and nothing more" penner
112 ___ favor (helps)
114 "Garfield" dog
116 Alleviated
118 Dog that likes to watch other dogs fight?
124 Judge in a TV title
125 Dog that likes to hang around soda fountains?
126 Go toe-to-toe with
127 "___ luck?"
128 Help in a heist
129 Oyster concoction

DOWN

1 Brit's raincoat
2 *Le dernier* ___ (the latest fashion)
3 Highway havens
4 Corfu's waters, the ___ Sea
5 Look up to
6 "___ reflection ..."
7 "Ransom" director Howard
8 American Airlines, on the NYSE
9 "Peanuts" character
10 Colleen
11 Apartment, e.g.
12 Noted diarist
13 Capital of Afghanistan
14 A Bergen dummy
15 Homeowner's payment: abbr.
16 Ripken Jr. and Sr.
17 What's what in Mexico?
19 Closer to the door?
20 Consumer
23 A long time
27 Chubby's dance
28 Actor Vaughn
29 "___ World Turns"
31 Mideast-summit attendees
32 Slangy mouth
33 Hatch from Utah
35 Really long time
36 Popular ending?
37 "___ available" (researcher's dead end)
38 Waste-watching org.
40 Thistlelike plant
41 Commercial slogan, e.g.
42 Salad choice
46 "I can't take it, but "you" can
47 Pants-leg bottom
50 It means "all"
51 Algerian port
52 Pizazz
53 Curly whacker
54 Hit song from "Tommy"
55 Pastrami parlor
59 1980 John Carpenter film
62 Voluminous ref. set
64 The Cardinals, on scoreboards
66 Volcano, at time
67 Bakery-cafe chain
68 Flap on a winter cap
69 McDonald's Corp. founder Ray
70 Hush-hush
72 Comet feature
73 One-eyed flirtation
74 Engrave
77 "... ___ quit!" (ultimatum ending)
80 Man with a law named after him
81 Half a fly
82 ___ diving
84 Mil. truants
86 Cup-shaped flower
87 "You're ___ talk!"
88 In ___ (stupefied)
90 Spanish bear
92 Scratch (out a living)
93 On the other side of the st. from
96 Latin 101 verb
99 Litigant
101 In a flimsy way
102 Horseshoe-shaped symbol
103 Get testy with
104 Rope fiber
105 Surgical tubes
107 Intimidate, with "out"
108 Skater Cohen
112 Floor model
113 African antelope
114 Sea predator
115 "My Heart Will Go On" singer
116 Salinger girl
117 Low-cal
118 Sharp left or right
119 Pea's keeper
120 Greek letter
121 Yank foe
122 Compass pt.
123 "Ben-Hur" author Wallace

ACROSS

1 Web site visits, in stat lingo
6 ___ of salt
11 Prism effects
18 Of a heart part
20 Anthony in "Psycho"
22 Reserve for Christmas, e.g.
23 Unsatisfied colony founder?
25 Frosty demarcation
26 Roughly speaking
27 Unsatisfied novelist?
29 Unsatisfied Hollywood makeup artist?
33 Rocky pinnacle
34 Passé: abbr.
35 ___ for effort
36 Grizzly, to Guzmán
37 "Maude" star
38 "... ___ my Romeo comes"
39 Richard Dysart series
42 Unsatisfied gagmeister?
50 Cloth and dry goods dealers, in Britain
53 Hyde Park dog
54 Destination of Apr. letters
55 Benefit
56 Unsatisfied chief exec?
60 ___ temperature
61 Chosen few
62 Welsh poet Thomas
63 ___ even keel
64 With 68 Across, unsatisfied canal guy?
68 See 64 Across
72 Excited
73 Greet cordially
77 Salon selection
78 "Dies ___"
79 Unsatisfied inventor?
84 Taping abbr.
85 Nogales cry
86 "Laugh-In" name
87 Turks' neighbors
89 Unsatisfied actress?
94 Peevish
95 Arts org.
96 Shoe size
97 Sleuth's shout
100 Nice round number
101 Na Na preface
102 French dance
103 Unsatisfied TV actress?
108 Unsatisfied film actress?
111 Dissipated guy
112 Render untraceable, as cash
113 Unsatisfied cartoonist?
118 Mise ___
119 Water spirit of Celtic myth
120 32-card card game
121 Utah, once
122 For ___ (cheaply)
123 Maya Angelou poem, "And Still ___"

DOWN

1 "Batman Forever" guy
2 "Am ___ understand ..."
3 Throw to the wrong base, e.g.
4 ___'s cruse (endless supply)
5 Khachaturian's "___ Dance"
6 Tiny carpenter
7 "Why ___ these things?"
8 Knight protection
9 Marshmallow creation
10 Part of a spy's name
11 More underhanded
12 Fund-raising grps.
13 City blights
14 .22, for one
15 Matched pair
16 Sounded (true)
17 "Will do"
19 Rodeo prop
21 Lipton rival, on hot days
24 Plenty
28 Gardening soil
29 Worn, as radials
30 Take guns from, variantly
31 The ___ Lama
32 Child-care expert
37 With 49 Down, "certainly!"
38 Sartre's "L'___ et le Neánt" ("Being and Nothingness")
40 Make ___ (support NPR or PBS)
41 "___ never!"
43 Competition ender
44 Attack
45 With May, a TV hillbilly
46 English title
47 "Rebel Rouser" guitarist Eddy
48 No sweat
49 See 37 Down
51 Drops from the sky
52 Sp. miss
57 Hard to see through, as fog
58 Magazine of Fold-In fame
59 Time allotted for lunch, usu.
60 1937 MGM musical with Cole Porter songs
64 Laissez ___
65 Bird found in Florida
66 Bug found everywhere
67 German article
69 G. Carroll and others
70 A Deadly Sin
71 Quick drink of booze
74 Brussels violinist Eugene
75 Ill-treatment
76 Lay ___ (upbraid)
79 Goya's duchess
80 Pastoral place, in poems
81 German article
82 Refinement
83 Joins the game
85 Poison-leaved shrub
88 Thesaurus items: abbr.
90 Augment
91 Paper amount
92 Secure anew
93 Common ache site
98 ___ de combat
99 Win by ___
101 Green eggs concocter
102 Green hat?
103 Licks and closes
104 He was unspeakably zany
105 "Candy" star Ewa
106 Aldo of fashion
107 Hungarian composer Franz
108 Junglefrau?
109 Bird of Hawaii
110 Bird of Argentina
112 Was winning
114 Brain scan: abbr.
115 Mr. Geller
116 PD ranks
117 Zuider ___

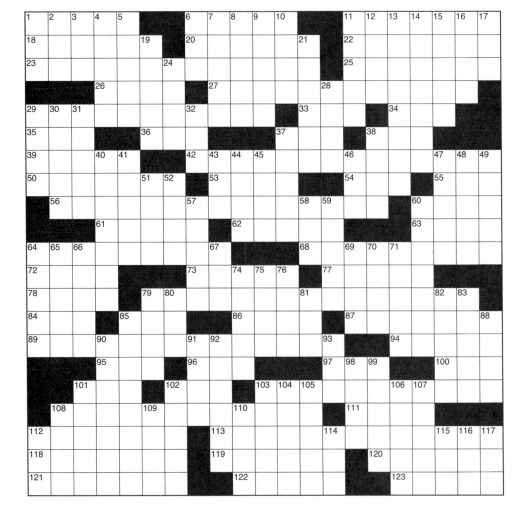

11 Are You Ready for Some Foodball?

...Food, yes; ball, no

ACROSS

1 Ronald's first Defense secretary
7 Foolish talk
13 Sno-cone kin
18 Glacial deposit
19 Old marketplaces
20 Image prefix
21 Loading up your plate on game day?
22 Much of Mauritania
23 Snow fortress
24 Completely
25 O.T. book
27 The rest of a submarine sandwich?
29 Whip up some homemade Cheez Whiz?
34 Imagist, e.g.
35 Dry gullies
36 Cup part
37 Grid fan's big chili order?
42 Financing abbr.
43 Swift
45 Choice: abbr.
46 Oft-dunked item
47 Add a little salt now before adding more salt later?
51 Well now
53 Elevate
54 ___ seed (deteriorate)
55 Icelandic work
57 Twixt sm. & lge.
58 Market currents
59 First name in pop art
60 School org.
61 Starlet's dream
63 "Analyze ___"
64 Willing word
65 Pounds put on by grid fans?
68 Place to do laps
71 Green, green grass of home
72 Small one
73 Pile-driver part
74 Fly high
75 Assumes to be true
78 Strain
79 Pipe part
81 In a bind
82 Ointment
83 Trees in a Respighi piece
85 Post-breakfast dish residue?
87 Feng ___
88 Mining find
89 Gave medicine to
91 Unconscious
92 Pastries for grid fans?
95 Small amount
96 Pacify
100 Stern-looking
101 Fish advertised on ESPN?
104 Had a lot of ketchup?
108 Tucson campus, briefly
109 Ofc. VIP
110 The sun, in Sonora
111 Tot tender
113 How post-game dieters should lose weight?
117 Barcelona boys
118 Full
119 Airline enticement
120 Make ___ for oneself
121 Was impudent
122 River cleaner

DOWN

1 Arrest
2 Agent Gold on HBO's "Entourage"
3 Salvador's intro
4 "Animal Farm" villain
5 Battery parts
6 Descartes et al.
7 Hallucinogenic nightmare
8 Get up there?
9 Nova opener?
10 Poodle, terrier, etc.
11 ___ de triomphe
12 Halted legally
13 Web designer
14 Switching centers of a sort
15 Troy Aikman alma mater, briefly
16 Small-runway aircraft
17 To walk (with "it")
18 Certain runner
21 Sunscreen abbr.
26 High ground
28 Christmasy name
30 Warm
31 Blood designation
32 Israeli folk dance
33 "The Lord of the Rings," for one
38 Like some books or cars
39 Algerian port
40 Fuse, in a way
41 Parking places
43 Toho pterodactyl of 1956
44 Mannequins
47 "Let us ___"
48 Ancient symbol
49 Outcomes
50 Take hold
52 Boating hazard
53 Galway's land, in song
56 Attached
58 The visiting players
60 Boxer's feet
62 Toward the rear
63 Buccaneers et al.
65 Way out
66 Yemen neighbor
67 Tire concern
68 Vinegary
69 Six-___
70 Bible vessels
71 Game-watching site, often
74 Liberty, for one
75 Attention-getter
76 Where Pearl is
77 Curved line, in music
78 Level
80 "Tommy" rockers
81 Flatten, slangily
83 Propositions, in logic
84 Lax
86 Great number
88 Roman poet
90 Locked down
93 Menacing words
94 Walter and Willard
96 "Do me ___"
97 Look up to
98 "___ with a spoon!"
99 Fictional governess
102 Slangy opponents
103 Gone by
104 Transportation secretary under Clinton
105 Actress Lena
106 Annapolis letters
107 "30 Rock" first name
112 Now or long preceder
114 Farm female
115 TV oldie, "Mayberry ___"
116 Price place

ACROSS

1 Neighbor of Mozambique
7 Slangy gossip
11 Booth's treater
15 Somewhat wet
19 Birth
20 Like a wing
21 De-fence-ive weapon?
22 "Stride la vampa," for one
23 Reaction to French art prices?
26 Suit option
27 Palindromic suffix
28 Reunification's Helmut
29 Gauguin's OK
30 Cheerios-box superlative
32 Painter Chagall
34 When the art museum is closed?
38 Troublesome tykes
41 Triumvirate total
42 Cul-___
43 "___ and Her Sisters"
46 Top rating, often
47 Sweat drops
49 Play critics?
53 Chicken's reaction to great art?
56 Khan's concern
58 Tiny tunneler
59 Harden
60 Letter-shaped add-on
61 Penultimate Greek letter
62 Bean Town team
63 Stir up
65 Mountain yield
66 Staring angrily
68 Famous fantasizer
70 Classic novel about a painter?
74 Painter Rivera
76 Apply oil to
77 "___ man of means by no means, king of the road"
78 Partly
81 Roman art
82 Nickname that's missing "art"
84 Infamous gun
85 Rudely sarcastic
87 Gina's "Solomon and Sheba" co-star
88 Character actor Regis
90 What you need to get into Paul's exhibit?
93 Eugene's Christie
94 Showy perennial
96 Ring site
97 What the clueless have
98 Baby kangaroos
100 Anagram of "art"
101 E-mail button
102 Reaction to American art prices?
108 Whack (a piggy)
112 Shore-related
113 Pal, to Seurat
114 Name in Hirschfeld artwork
117 Uracil-based acid
118 Basket alternative
119 Two guys famous for their oils?
124 "That's ___ need!"
125 Jacob's brother
126 Oil container
127 Barbra classic
128 A gender: abbr.
129 Hit the malls
130 Web ___
131 Go over

DOWN

1 Computer peripheral
2 Sports venue
3 Jungle cat hybrid
4 Turkish title
5 "Ring around the collar" brand
6 Penetrating preposition
7 First name in cubist art
8 Festive cry
9 Symbol of strength
10 A ___ (in theory)
11 Newspapers, radio, etc.
12 Wire service
13 Signified
14 Neutralizes a magnetic field
15 Tennis prize
16 Thin as ___
17 "You don't ___ trick, do you?"
18 Beefcake?
24 Resistance units
25 Charge that makes MADD mad
31 Sri Lankan export
33 Five, to Manet
35 Agnes, to Cecil B.
36 Drop shot, in tennis
37 Fargo's st.
39 Island on Auau Channel
40 DiMag, in his day
43 Metal beam
44 River in Tuscany
45 1940 Richard Wright novel
46 Big soup dish
47 Item in Barney Fife's shirt pocket
48 Acclaim
50 Weepy
51 Luth. or Meth.
52 Like the covers of Cosmopolitan
54 Part of FBI
55 Showy houseplant
57 Chevalier song
61 Hunting document
64 Table support
66 In ___ (excited)
67 "Misery" director
69 "___ no use"
71 One of 7 Down's artistic "periods"
72 City on the Seine
73 Nobelist Gordimer
74 Polling results, e.g.
75 Essential mineral
79 Tone down, as colors
80 Sam thinks she's bad luck
83 Font features
85 Part of Ringo's kit
86 Subj. for an MBA
89 Truly grand
90 Micro or macro addition
91 Close
92 Many a family's pride and joy
95 Pain in the peeper
99 Frequently, briefly
100 Flashy Fords, familiarly
101 Forget (it)
102 The "simplest is best" principle, ___'s razor
103 Eucalyptus-leaf lover
104 Grey and Holliman
105 "Finish your food!"
106 Latin lover's word
107 You ___
109 Figure of speech
110 Cecil B., to Agnes
111 Potato preference
115 Casual negative
116 "Jeopardy!" guy
120 ___ Paulo
121 Christina's dad
122 Brazil, for one
123 Spot: abbr.

NOTE: *Hidden in this grid (once it's filled in) are six types of pirate treasure, all written in an uninterrupted, straight line, but diagonally. Can you dig up all six?*

ACROSS

1 Legendary pirate Gaspar
5 British sports cars
8 Sot's woe
11 Old joke: Q. "What does a ___ pirate cut out of his diet?" A. "Larrrrrd"
14 "Old MacDonald had ___"
16 Like a pirate fight, usually
17 Pirate spoils
18 Not ___ (only okay)
20 Site of Captain Kidd's first act of piracy
21 Author Hubbard
22 Two-toed sloth
23 "It's only ___"
24 Views with disdain, pirate-style?
27 London pealer
28 Historic time
29 Mel the Giant
30 Slippery seagoer
31 Actress Grier
34 Author Rand
35 With 59 Across, "Help!"
36 Sports org. N of the border
37 Mantra syllables
40 Treasure, e.g.
42 Young one
43 Young one
44 Do recon work
46 "Don't be ___!"
47 Famed Wall St. index: abbr.
49 Mandela's land, officially: abbr. (anagram of 79 Across)
50 Jim Hawkins thwarts one in a pirate classic
51 Longtime hotbed of piracy
53 "High" place for piracy
54 Pines
55 Snake eyes
56 Polish name for a Ukrainian city (no, it's not the French word for "Awesome!")
57 Menus, in Paris
59 See 35 Across
60 Bull's opposite
61 Some neckwear
63 Old Ford models
65 Fisherman's name?
67 More prying
69 Henry VIII's quest
70 Asian holiday
73 Sean's first "Bond girl"
75 Replacements for some pirates?
76 Freebooter
78 Black or red pirate features
79 ___ longa, vita brevis
80 German philosopher
81 Divided nation
82 Gets outta there
83 Flynn's Peter Blood et al.: abbr.
84 Beer holder
85 Like pirates, often
86 Mil. training prog.
87 Home, for ex.
88 Give, as odds
89 Plane peril, ___ piracy
91 Yes, to a pirate
92 Day before
93 Scoundrel
94 Greek letter
95 They go with crossbones
99 Car inspired by pirates?
107 Errol's pirate co-star, 1935
108 Ship direction
109 Tolstoy and others
110 Jolly ___
111 Confused, pirate-style?
112 Damsel
113 Really big show
114 Country oft-targeted by pirates
115 Hosp. areas
116 Had a feast
117 Network: abbr.
118 Patron saint of sailors

DOWN

1 Where pirates may end up
2 ___ consequence
3 ___-masochists
4 Composer Satie
5 English pirate, Henry ___
6 Pirate quaff
7 "Auld Lang ___"
8 "The Count of Monte Cristo" star
9 Perfectly
10 Cook's name?
11 Verne's circumnavigator
12 Captain of The Pequod
13 Big book
15 More, to Moreno
16 Harshly bright
17 Wench-hungry, as pirates
18 Travel like a pirate
19 Usual number of paces
25 "15 men on a ___ man's chest ..."
26 Line on a map
27 De Maupassant's "___-Ami"
30 Salamander
31 "Fiddlesticks!"
32 Old Olds
33 Husband, in Lyon
35 Actress Farrow
36 The Barbary ___
37 Double foursomes
38 Actress Shearer
39 Bright
40 "Why do ___ this way?"
41 Count, for example
42 Relatives
43 Old Russian rulers
44 Take to court
45 Cobb et al.
47 Area of Western Sahara, Rio ___ (anagram of RODEO)
48 Bone with teeth attached to it
49 English lady pirate, Mary ___
50 Connecticut port
52 Safari bosses
53 Pirate face features
58 Vote in
60 Says suddenly
61 Coffin stands
62 Brain tests: abbr.
64 Sir Francis, whom many considered a pirate
65 Painter El ___
66 Ishmael's half-brother
68 Rigging supports
69 Attila was one
70 Old comic strip, "___ and the Pirates"
71 Really big shoe
72 Conventional, as folk mus.
73 The network in "Network"
74 Mormon inits.
76 Booty container
77 Weather org.
80 Chest opener
83 Actress Sandra
84 Unfunny Marx
85 Herr's other half
87 Campers
88 Pirate's favorite instruments?
89 ___ Fables
90 Ronstadt's "___ Easy"
92 Singer Fitzgerald
93 Treasure hunter's worry
95 Org. for entrepreneurs
96 Shakespearean shrew
97 Old map letters
98 Falsehoods
99 Winter wear
100 Pirate quaffs
101 Like Johnny Depp, perhaps
102 7, on old phones
103 Hanging requirement
104 On a par, in Paris
105 "Take ___ Yours"
106 Cube man Rubik
108 1 Across's home turf, today: abbr.

14 | Hard-To-Do Songs

...Only if you're literal-minded

ACROSS

1 Roughage
6 He dressed Grace and Marilyn
10 Datebook datum: abbr.
14 Tailor's concern
17 Enter a soapbox derby?
18 Experience anew
21 Good sign?
22 Boll's I
23 1958 hit song ("okay, but it won't be easy")
26 Reed you can read
27 Mind numbers
28 Love god
29 Swan lady
30 Part of DOS
32 1965 hit song ("okay, but it won't be easy")
36 Petal perfumes
39 "___ impossible"
40 Ingot stuff, in Barcelona
41 "Chinatown" gumshoe
42 "___ am a sinful man" (Luke 5:8)
43 Certain noncom: abbr.
45 In a nimble manner
48 Afternoon affair
49 1954 song ("okay, but it won't be easy")
53 Malingerers
55 "Xanadu" band
56 N.Y.C. tourist attraction
57 Remove dowels (from)
59 Most egregious
60 Decennial event
62 Louisiana soups
65 St. Louis to Louisville
67 What dendro- means
68 1955 hit song ("okay, but it won't be easy")
71 O'Hara's home
75 Green-curry cuisine
77 Scold
78 Drove (along)
80 Furrow
83 Warm coat
85 Brat's target
87 Witness words
88 Dean of bestsellers
90 1991 rock tune ("okay, but it won't be easy")
94 Agcy. estab. in 1862
95 Joan of Arc's crime
97 Bills
98 Climactic opening?
99 Spoil a surprise
101 D.C. type
102 Anat., e.g.
103 Cleans quickly
105 1992 pop song ("okay, but it won't be easy")
111 Banquet
112 Swedish name that's an Indian name backwards
113 Jason's ship
114 Identity query
117 Mustard's rank: abbr.
118 1959 show tune ("okay, but it won't be easy")
122 Online address, familiarly
123 Fishing need
124 Appeared
125 Ahead of time
126 -ish alternative
127 MIT grad, perh.
128 Roanoke's Virginia
129 Hope for addicts

DOWN

1 Ellipse-determining points
2 Site of a 2007 surge
3 Is up
4 Catchall abbr.
5 Listen to again, as a case
6 "Friend ___?"
7 Lion's share's opposite
8 Building wing
9 Blade maker
10 Hot tub sounds
11 Touches repeatedly with a towel
12 Hit the links
13 Body section
14 Hooch, humorously
15 Fridge features
16 Abbreviation of appreciation
19 Opinions
20 Within: pref.
24 Bible vessels
25 Needlefish
31 Mausoleum's front?
32 Mangle
33 Like the sky
34 Guy on the Ponderosa set
35 It's a rising thing
36 Influence
37 Bell ringer
38 "Have a piece!"
43 Soccer ___
44 Stiffly theatrical
45 Mexican state
46 ___ up (hits a shallow fly)
47 Oscillates, as a projectile
50 Outback sight
51 Opera about a diva
52 Egyptian bigwig
54 Actor Yaphet
58 "No kiddin'!"
61 Take hold
63 Eclipse shadows
64 In a mousy way
66 Larry's producer on "The Larry Sanders Show"
69 Tear
70 Sleeveless garments
72 Saucer people
73 Time-stamp anew
74 Aphrodite loved him
76 Bible verb
79 The woman in the song "Woman"
80 Flees (town)
81 Bullfighters, once
82 City NE of Sacramento
84 Deep as ___
86 LBJ VP
89 The Hindenburg, e.g.
91 Transpired
92 Neet rival
93 Some six-packs
96 Like the '20s
100 Author Kesey
102 Dry white Italian wine
103 Tomato sauce brand
104 Straightened (out)
106 Remus, e.g.
107 Brief freedom?
108 Actor Montand
109 Person with a whip
110 Wear away
114 ___ hog
115 Hawaiian city
116 Cameo stone
117 Prompt
119 Cousteau's milieu
120 Singer Sumac
121 ___ kwon do

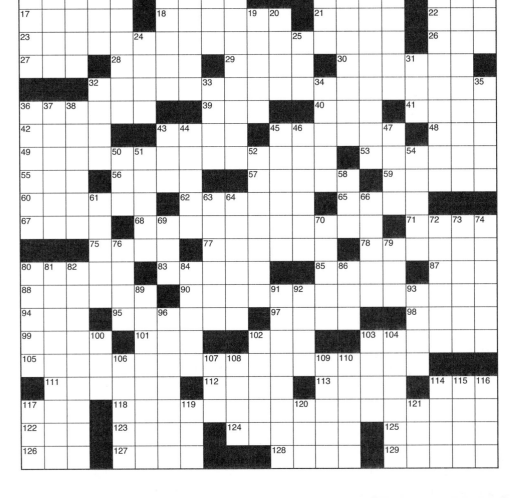

NOTE: *Here's a pretty straight-forward puzzle about one of Hollywood's greatest and most enduring stars. And the diagram contains four hints to the star's identity — **even before you start solving.** If you can't figure out what the four hints are, they're revealed on the puzzle's solution page.*

ACROSS

1 Highlander
5 Long-range weapon
9 Helen's "What Women Want" co-star
12 Bees
18 Arch type
19 Behave like an ass
20 Base for bacteria
22 Bela Fleck plays them
23 History Channel topics
24 Safe-streets org.
25 Tonic starter
26 Creature whose coat changes
27 Enter ender
28 The Tappan ___ Bridge
29 Plane, on a screen
30 ___ lily
31 1970 drama
37 David Janssen series in which he played a detective
38 Capri has a famous one
39 "Bali ___"
40 Zoo denizen
43 When some coll. classes meet
45 1965 drama
48 Scottish hillside
51 Formerly, once
54 Calendar divs.
55 Actress Deborah
56 1957 epic
61 Infiniti rival
62 One way to run
63 Of wings
64 You can do it on your side
65 Bovary, e.g.: abbr.
67 1951 sequel to a 1950 classic
75 It's a sign
76 Peace, in Pskov
77 Actress Celeste
78 People from the year 802,701
79 Gets stubborn
83 1951 drama
86 Here, to Hernando
87 Field goo
89 Actress Russo
90 Ali Khamenei's land
91 1960 drama
96 Dodge model
98 Nickname of baseball Hall of Famer Carl
99 Actor Johnson
100 Luminosity
103 Dash cousins
108 1978 musical
111 Gettysburg general
114 Night flyers
115 Fidel friend, once
116 "Swoosh" company
117 Whirlwind
118 Form droplets
119 Quite a lot, as portions go
121 Prepare to bear it
122 Cat or goat
123 95 Down's river
124 Secluded spot
125 Location
126 Chinese religion
127 Reagan aide Nofziger
128 School for princes
129 Eur. airline

DOWN

1 Accompany
2 Mystery dame
3 More macabre
4 Complex individual?
5 Tech titan
6 Very hectic
7 No-goodnik
8 "Frankly, ___ ..."
9 Gory story
10 1/3 of a French rallying cry
11 Telemundo folks
12 Andy's predecessor
13 Root veggie
14 "Believe ___"
15 Dance ___
16 Rule-breaker
17 Walk this way?: abbr.
21 Engrossed
32 Shea player, once: abbr.
33 Stove setting
34 Slogan
35 Panicked plaint
36 Large amounts
40 Top
41 Andean land
42 Is human?
44 "You Make Me ___ Young"
46 Poet Lowell
47 Cold War leader
48 The Crimson Tide, briefly
49 One way to run
50 "Enduring life" symbol
52 Not a movie
53 Economize
56 High-flying organisation: abbr.
57 Special
58 Extreme
59 Nonexistent
60 Tyke's laugh
61 It'll ring your neck
65 "Adam-12" star
66 Occupy Wall St, e.g.: abbr.
68 They loop the Loop
69 No later than
70 Slay
71 Bambi, e.g.
72 "Born Free" lion
73 Part of speech
74 Clangor
79 Infant
80 Blue shade
81 Ice maneuver
82 Hobby-store buy
83 Retired female boxer Laila ___
84 General Abrams, written license-plate-style
85 Athlete's greeting
87 Pencilless test
88 Region of SW Morocco
92 Tax cheats
93 Indulge a healthy appetite
94 Soothing song
95 Rebuilt German city
97 Counter finish?
101 "All Night Long" singer
102 Shocked
104 Inspiring subjects?
105 Egyptian god
106 Cold War leader
107 Stage sequences
109 Bride-___
110 "Anybody here?"
111 Actress Freeman
112 Hence
113 Yours, in Tours
117 Big container
120 Marsh

16 Paul's Puzzle

...Words and music

NOTE: *I made this puzzle in June 2006 in honor of Paul McCartney's 64th birthday, since his classic tune "When I'm 64" was finally coming true for Paul himself. Every theme answer is a Beatles song on which Paul sang lead. Amazingly, every song also happens to be related to crossword puzzles. What are the chances?*

ACROSS

1 Miami's loc.
5 King supporter
13 Troubles
17 Neighborhoods
19 Pain in the brain
20 Gets together
22 Paul's crossword credo?
24 Bit of info
25 Ready
26 Arg. belongs to it
27 Time unit: abbr.
28 Square-dance verb
29 Groucho role, ___ T. Firefly
31 FBI guys
33 Ship part
35 Little jerk?
36 With 44 Across, where Paul solves crosswords?
38 Discover by chance
39 ___ choy

40 Food regimen
41 Chinese concept
42 Played for a fool
43 Ball belles
44 See 36 Across
48 Leave speechless
50 Chopper
51 Place for a ring?
52 Decked out
56 Quick-witted
59 Gentle ___
62 Kent portrayer
63 Paul's comment to a young befuddled solver?
66 Varnish resin
67 Beer-maker's sugar
68 Stand for something?
69 Hairsplitters
71 Lucy of "Charlie's Angels" (2000)
72 Mattress problem
73 Highest
74 Paul's all-over-the-grid solving style?
81 Wise men
84 ___ board
86 Aficionado
87 It's often added to a million
88 "Rules ___ rules"
89 Party poopers
90 When Paul last solved a puzzle?

93 Interest meas.
94 Oklahoma city
95 Large amount: slang
97 Garden tools
98 Where *une idée* originates
100 Ovine sound
101 Certain sib
102 Baby barker
104 Proclamation
105 Prior to 90 Across, when Paul last solved a puzzle?
110 Ever ___
111 Harangue
112 Flats and spikes
113 Maturing agent
114 Site of the Houdini Museum
115 In addition

DOWN

1 Cutting tools
2 No restrictions
3 Spoke at a seminar
4 Battery type
5 Greek letters
6 Poet's contraction
7 Talk a lot
8 Stop on ___
9 Liturgy language
10 Enduring symbol
11 Mu ___ pork

12 Asian holiday
13 Paul's feeling when he's stumped, no pun intended?
14 Pastoral places
15 Paul's warning to anyone touching his puzzle?
16 Daytime Fox News show
18 Animal nose
21 Painters' duds
23 Laundry
28 Thingy
30 Gala
31 Overcast
32 Siamese remark
33 Prop for Sherlock
34 Hwy., e.g.
36 Term for any region of packed-together people: abbr.
37 Raison d'___
38 Triumphant cries
42 Excludes from a hand
43 Jeter and Jacobi
45 Critter
46 Really big show
47 With enthusiasm
49 Writer's tally
52 ___ Dhabi
53 A goose on the island
54 Darwin's thing: abbr.
55 Drops at dawn
56 Only
57 Tinted
58 Designer Giorgio
59 "I solved it!"
60 Strangelove portrayer
61 Shemp's brother
63 "You betcha!"
64 Corporate IDs
65 Security problem
70 ___ and only
72 Grounded planes
74 Take note of
75 Irish pop star
76 Regretted
77 Merry escapade
78 Shoreline mini-pond
79 Wipeouts?
80 Marina Del ___
81 Sugar sources
82 1993 Tom Stoppard play
83 With 89 Down, Paul's modest wish as a solver?
85 Diagnostic option
89 See 83 Down
91 Paper name, briefly
92 Moves gingerly
95 Pole star?
96 Stone landmark
99 Behold, to Brutus
100 Tolerate
101 British gun
103 Jalisco coin
105 NFL stats
106 Juice-drink brand
107 Kin of "scat!"
108 It aired "Deadwood"
109 Mortgage org.

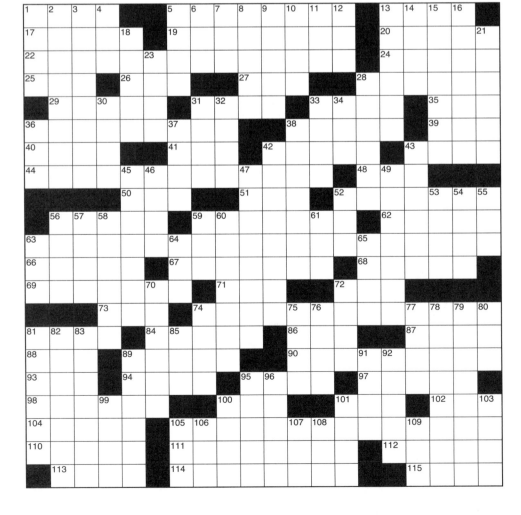

17 I Now Pronounce You ... Differently

...You said it

ACROSS

1 Shower-deprived
5 Volts ÷ amps
9 Solid-rock center?
12 Guys with gushers
18 ___ wanted to ___ the peace process
21 By now
22 ___ ___ life into his "Opus" cartoons
23 Put a hold on
24 Harry's follower
25 Poet's pasture
26 OH player
27 Roman crowd?
28 Three-player card game
29 You can answer this: abbr.
31 NASA vehicle
34 Reversal
37 Miss after the ceremony?
38 ___ was cast as an ___
42 Director Craven
43 Imitated
45 Away from the wind
46 Introduction to physics
47 Erstwhile Kudrow co-star
48 Great divides
50 Palindrome portion
52 Designer Mizrahi
54 Go after
55 Bit of machine-gun fire?
56 ___ liked to ___ his feet
61 Carol addition
62 Recipient
63 "Vive" follower
64 Win by ___
66 Melted *glace*
68 Ring immortal
69 ___ had a painful ___ to do
70 Amt. for Emeril
72 Regal letters
73 Good ___
75 Ablaze, to Pascal
77 Poker challenge
79 Crayola shade
80 ___ drove a ___ to the festival
84 Serve up a whopper
87 More lean and mean
89 Knocker's words
90 John Irving hero
92 Horseshoe-shaped letters
93 Caps lock, for one
94 "Don't ___ innocent"
97 Wind in a pit
98 Barnyard cry
99 King of Moo in "Alley Oop"
100 ___ of 'N Sync had a skinny wallet; now he has a ___
102 Bit of utilitarian art
103 "Oh puh-lease!"
107 Union foe
108 Day 5, usu.
109 H.H. Munro's alias
111 In stores
112 Popular hymn, with 33 Down
114 CPA's boom time
116 Pi follower
119 Donahue and Wylie
121 Monaco's ___ preferred ___ weather
125 Digital count?
126 ___ had a new security system ___
127 Newsman Charles
128 Freight weight
129 Twilight time
130 Sleuth Wolfe

DOWN

1 It means "both"
2 Be terrible, slangily
3 Falling back
4 N. or S. state
5 "___ still!"
6 Trumpets
7 Curie title: abbr.
8 Face on a silver dollar: inits.
9 Turkish bigwigs
10 It won't hold water
11 Far-away filler?
12 Olive oil's ___ acid
13 Treasury org.
14 Wine sediment
15 ___ played a ___ game of hockey than usual
16 ___ liked to ___ on fish while he painted
17 Dmitri's denials
19 Yo-Yo's string
20 Time-saving abbr.
21 Some songs
27 Wild goat
30 Watched warily
32 Treater at the scene
33 See 112 Across
35 Like some garages
36 Hilo honcho
38 Canter, e.g.
39 Mater intro
40 Thin layer
41 Snifter sniffer
44 Course figure
47 Biblical spy
48 Coast Guard noncom
49 Go after
51 "I love," to Ovid
53 "The pleasure is ___"
57 Fanzine focus
58 "Die Lorelei" poet
59 "___ I see you first"
60 Punk rock was a reaction to it
62 Expected
65 Senators' org.
66 ___ says that ___ just as important as talent on a movie set
67 ___ would rather be dancing than ___ her stamp pads
69 Breakwater
71 Included in
73 Part of Welk's intro
74 Inflicts
76 Parthenon feature
78 The Mormons, initially
81 IV sites
82 Certain mus. key
83 Style of furnishing
84 Tony Blair, e.g.
85 Straighten (out)
86 Duel tool
88 Car starter: abbr.
91 Teutonic invader
93 Goldie's longtime guy
95 Kicker's prop
96 Ancient city whose name gave us a word meaning "hedonist"
99 German math whiz
101 Take ___ (travel)
102 Be of ___ (help)
104 Scrutinized, with "over"
105 Danny's daughter
106 Aquafina rival
110 Fascinated by
113 Nip in the bud
115 Place to stroll
117 Next in line
118 "Yes ___?"
120 Resetting setting
121 Mil. rank
122 El ___
123 Down Under runner
124 Agnes of "Agnes of God," e.g.

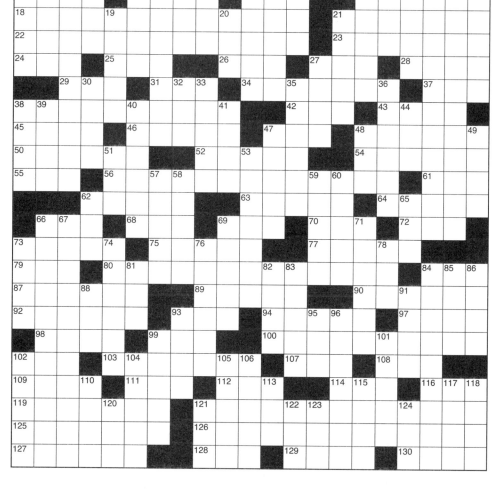

18 Where Am I?

...We're thinking of expanding

NOTE: *The eight theme answers are hiding things — in order of size, more or less.*

ACROSS

1 Navy noncoms
5 Miler's path
9 The Beehive State
13 Mayberry's self-incarcerator
17 Inventor's middle name
18 Judge's coverup?
19 Dressy doings
21 Khartoum's land
23 Max Jr. who played TV's Jethro
24 Witch of the comics
26 Pilfered
27 Rugged rock
29 Albacore et al.
30 Site for a safe
32 Windows alternative
33 Dashboard dial
35 Kentucky college
36 Editor's order
37 ___ glance
38 Put a strain on
39 Compete
41 Killer whale
43 Play about Capote
44 Largo and lento, e.g.
46 Dual deal of a sort
50 They're out of your mind
51 Convent
52 African antelope
53 Violinist's first name
55 Thick-as-thieves types
57 "Driving Miss Daisy" star
60 "What nerve!"
63 It may get agitated
66 Hawaii's Mauna ___
67 Rain heavily
68 Up
69 Proclamation
71 Exec's "now"
72 Carry-on item
73 Swiss artist Paul
74 Noted "paparazzi magnet"
77 Like Captain Ahab
79 Leave port
81 Stevie Wonder's "My ___ Amour"
82 Calls it a day
85 "To Love Somebody" group
87 Pipers' wear
91 "I think I misdealt"
94 Friendly
95 Mr. Parseghian
96 Pony poker
97 M.p.g. rater
98 Recyclable item
99 Tackle moguls
100 Source of zest
102 "Lohengrin" aria, "___ Dream"
104 Crushed
108 Oz visitor
109 Self-satisfied
110 Man of La Mancha, for example
111 Old name for a dairy stick
112 "My Fair Lady" girl
114 Detached feeling
117 Stats and such
119 Get in the way of
120 Word form for "sleep"
121 Singer Fitzgerald
122 "Death of a Salesman" son
123 Lip-___
124 Leisurely
125 Hoarse voice
126 Technical sch.

DOWN

1 Hotel waiter?
2 Mollified
3 Beat
4 Vaughan of jazz
5 Space ball?
6 Whirlpool, e.g.
7 In reference to
8 Sierra ___
9 Disgusted grunts
10 ___ chi
11 "___ are saying ..."
12 Argued (with)
13 WWII spy org.
14 Skimpy skirts
15 Doubting words
16 "Amadeus" role
20 Italian seaport
22 "Coming after the break ..."
25 "Cat Ballou" co-star
28 Leave port
31 Shoestring tier
33 "Mon Oncle" star Jacques
34 More, in Madrid
35 Back-stabber
40 Klutzy
42 The "R" that starts with an A: abbr.
45 Check writer
46 Back-stabbers
47 Getting cold
48 Toothpick Olive?
49 Start-up helper: abbr.
51 Type of film with no costume designer?
54 Throw hard
56 Nothing-but-net baskets
58 Acheson or Rusk
59 Slangy mouth
60 Perfectly
61 Boatload, e.g.
62 Unassembled
64 Flu symptoms
65 Move a little
67 "NewsHour" network
70 Like omelet ham
71 Dined at home
73 Gentle cycle items
75 ___ of faith
76 Compare with
78 Hose wrecker
80 Like some dicts.
83 Varieties
84 Sam and Dave hit
86 Top-notch
88 Eavesdrop on
89 Spoofs
90 Lost traction
91 Hauled
92 Losers to the 1969 Miracle Mets
93 Writer Le Guin et al.
94 Station's supply
98 Seasonal songs
101 Carton count
103 "It's ___!"
105 Stage direction
106 Cousin of "presto!"
107 Suspect's story
110 Chilly powder?
113 Pop fly's path
115 Earth-friendly prefix
116 Short time-out
118 Repeatedly, briefly

...I already pulled the switch

ACROSS

1 Gauchos' ropes
7 Word on a map of Uzbekistan
11 Wrote wrong, e.g.
17 Sitcom about a family of tobacco chewers?
19 Thinker Descartes
20 Diamond authority
21 Fat guy's excuse?
23 Director Soderbergh
24 Outboard backup
25 Metrics opener
26 Brit. ref. work
27 Muckraker's first name
29 Turquoise relative
31 Response to being proposed to in the rain?
37 Listless
41 Malarial symptom
42 Like babes and hunks
43 Most popular show on the All Fungus Network?
49 Hemming need
50 Prop ending
51 Juan's "ones"
52 Island where Homer is reputedly buried
53 Like some nests
55 Bygone despots
57 Didn't work
60 A miner test?
63 A Mother and others
65 Confession of a rock band who played great individually but lousy as a group?
70 Put in place, as cable
71 Ben, away from the Ponderosa
73 New car of 1957
74 Gang ___
75 Chef known for his broccoli-and-bean dishes?
78 Type of blanket
80 Living quarters
81 Kept tabs on a friend's tabby
83 Perspective
84 "L.A. Confidential" co-star
87 Comic-strip yip
88 Hospital concerns
90 Danger to divers
91 Short flight
92 Twosome who were just too much?
99 Don of talk radio
101 Bar between wheels
102 You can't hear if you're out of it
103 What the extras were in "The Story of Xerxes"?
107 Shoebox number
111 Neighbors of the sopranos, perhaps
112 Recent USNA grad
113 "Pygmalion" monogram
116 Office-seeker, briefly
117 Where you might see FALCO LAVIN HESTON CAGNEY
120 With 127 Across, bio of a noted singer-actor?
125 Hurting
126 Printing process, briefly
127 See 120 Across
128 Moistens, as meat
129 Strong as ___
130 Key rings?

DOWN

1 Corduroy feature
2 Fancy sewing case
3 Does something
4 Bandleader Puente
5 Grabbed something on the way
6 Damascus is its cap.
7 Ram's sign
8 ___-Wip
9 Singer DiFranco
10 "___ then, you and I ..." (from "The Love Song of J. Alfred Prufrock")
11 Not-to-be-missed
12 "Honestly, ___ tired"
13 Lays out
14 The AL East, for ex.
15 Cork's loc.
16 Habitable hole
17 Ex-B-ball star, for short
18 There's a vicuna on its flag
21 ___ large extent
22 "What ___ now?"
28 Come down in buckets
30 Pub order
31 Oklahoma oil center
32 Concealed
33 Suckers
34 Actor Johnny
35 Way out
36 Wall St.'s loc.
38 "What ___!" ("Wimp!")
39 Lead-in to lethal
40 Ages
43 Turkey feature
44 Slacks measure
45 Affectionate nickname
46 Poodle's name
47 Least loud
48 Global septet
54 Eager player's cry
56 Sketch from scratch
58 Done vocals
59 4,840 square yards
60 Spam, mostly
61 Suffers in August, perhaps
62 Actress Ward
64 French phone greeting
66 Ben & Jerry's rival
67 Orbital extreme
68 "Whether 'tis ___ ..."
69 Prepares to propose
72 Actress Charlotte
76 "A likely story!"
77 Where Mandela was pres.
79 Anti follower
82 Lat. and long., e.g.
84 Fashionable
85 Type of tomato
86 Symphony, say
87 Say positively
89 "What was I thinking?!"
93 Is quick
94 Really big show
95 Big name in fake fat
96 Car contract
97 PBS chef of "Can Cook" fame
98 Area of S.F., Pacific ___
100 Take a ___ (try)
104 Kate's TV pal
105 Take care of
106 Tray containing work to do
108 ___ dixit
109 They feature creatures
110 Little mischief-maker
113 Greek deli order
114 Round-ending sound
115 Clipper feature
117 Type of 115 Down
118 Merkel or O'Connor
119 Base cops
121 Darlin'
122 Org. for entrepreneurs (or backwards, tummy muscles)
123 Boy king
124 Parkers at KOA sites

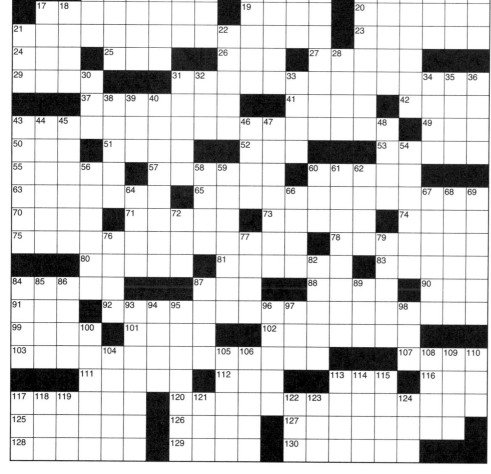

ACROSS

1 "Of course," slangily
6 Sand holder
10 Network on the 118 Down
13 Put on the line
17 In reserve
18 Invalidate
20 Prepare, as tuna
21 Athlete for whom ESPN's Courage Award is named
22 Early sitcom co-star
24 Hittites' home
26 Latin I word
27 Rep. or Sen.
28 Wall Street whiz
30 Slangy money
32 ___ Alamos
34 Naturalness
35 New Haven student
36 "Instant reporting"
41 1951 PGA champ
45 Quite a feller?
46 Ring leader, once
47 Crew with eggs-perience
49 Humane org.
50 New Age musician
53 RNA has it; DNA doesn't
56 President's nickname
58 "___ magic!"
59 Dye family
60 Chef's meas.
62 Famed victory speech
66 Nursery supplies
68 Canty, the pauper
70 Useless, as a battery
71 Ball honoree
72 Wildcats' home
79 With 80 Across, a court gaffe
80 See 79 Across
81 WWII command
82 Ostracize
84 1964 musical about a race car driver named Lucky Jackson
89 Hole maker
91 Judge at home
92 Buddy, before Barnaby
93 ___ room
94 Alex Trebek word
96 Actress Samantha
98 La Salle of "ER"
100 Spoken fanfare
103 Opening words of "Travelin' Man"
104 Prelude to a kiss
105 Type of rifle
107 Source of flow woes
113 One of the Cyclades
115 Bucks intro
116 The Cenozoic, e.g.
117 Type option
119 Term for Czechoslovakia's peaceful breakup in 1993
125 Hosp. staffers
127 Not sm.
128 Now playing, as movies
129 Czechoslovakia's leader before its breakup
132 It stinks
133 Ogler
134 First name in Vermont history
135 Bikini, for one
136 Camera part
137 Number of letters in *sí*
138 Film on Santa?
139 Untidy

DOWN

1 Political columnist Robert
2 20 Questions question
3 Site of the Villa d'Este
4 3 x LXVII
5 Junker
6 Dog studier
7 Baptist intro
8 Some stopovers
9 Vito's 77 Down
10 Surround, in a way
11 Barbara who played Cinnamon Carter on TV's "Mission: Impossible"
12 Desire strongly
13 Trail mix ingredients
14 Ain't as it should be?
15 Wave (away)
16 "The King and I" co-star
19 Embankment
20 Obeys a doctor's order
23 "Affliction" star
25 "Alice" diner
29 Altern. sp.
31 Author ___ S. Connell
33 Operation souvenir
37 Get off the road
38 Norwegian king
39 Squad's concern
40 Arthurian lady
42 Gargantuan
43 Play opening
44 Court VIPs
48 No place to be somebody
50 Slangy mouth
51 Sea N of the Black Sea
52 Words of denial
53 Gang ___ (combine against)
54 Yield to desire
55 Property claim
57 Times to call, in ads
61 Hollywood hopeful
63 Virtuoso rock guitarist Steve
64 "If I Knew You Were Comin' ___ Baked a Cake"
65 Wading bird
67 Pole, for one
69 Huge turnouts
73 Prevaricator
74 Hebrew letter
75 Orders akin to porters
76 Utah, *par exemple*
77 Henchman
78 Arizona county
83 Home of "Weekend Edition"
84 Action word
85 1967 hit, "___ Rock and Roll Music"
86 USNA, e.g.
87 Landed
88 Big hauler
90 Swan lady
92 Civil War's Stuart
95 Bat's digs
97 Use clubs at clubs
99 Arrow cases
101 Passings
102 Run ___ (get sick)
104 Son of Czar Alexis I
106 Coward of note
108 Bighead's problem
109 Whittle
110 Straying
111 Swedish autos
112 Marx collaborator
114 Noble mount
118 British "box"
119 Bass ___
120 "The Neverending Story" author, ironically
121 Author Hubbard
122 Belafonte refrain
123 Lloyd Webber hit
124 Repeat
126 Phony deal
130 Pathet ___
131 Feasted

21 Like, Totally Jazzed

...Music that sounds a little funny

ACROSS

1 Paper name, briefly
5 "The Nightmare Before Christmas" hostage
10 "Band of Gold" singer Payne
15 Four-legged William Powell co-star
19 Quickie divorce mecca
20 Puccini pieces
21 Better equipped
22 Windows alternative
23 Jazz guitarist's admission?
26 Agatha title
27 More, to Mario
28 Visibility hindrance
29 Musical Mama
30 Tear at the same spot
32 Sell in a hurry
34 Shindig or wingding
35 Window shopper's buy?
36 Word oft-repeated in "96 Tears"
39 Bike and bridle, e.g.
40 What lifelong jazz musicians are?
43 Fish delicacy
44 "Boom-de-ay" opener
46 Fork site
47 Mo or Stew of 6 Down
49 Sphere preceder
52 Mtn. stats
54 A kinder, gentler notion
55 Sgt. Friday's introduction
56 Name for a jazz club?
59 City near Hackensack
61 "10" piece
62 Gull's nesting place, often
64 Sandwich on toast
65 Big name in skis and snowboards
68 Hand communication: abbr.
69 Play clarinet?
74 Jeff Lynne's grp.
75 Hot-foot cry
77 "Everybody knows that!"
78 The Fates, e.g.
79 Walk or talk aimlessly
81 Surveillance option
84 Jazz crooner?
87 Large evergreen, ironically
89 Bus. card datum
91 Poker move
92 Units with a mgr.
93 Hatch's first
94 The Auld Sod
95 Hit hard
97 Org. involved in the healthcare debate
98 Where to buy jazz instruments?
102 Awaken rudely
106 Barnyard butter
107 New Haven alumni
108 Headed for overtime
109 Dorm sharer
110 Books review
112 Tomato variety
113 Lose traction
115 Author Deighton
116 Smoker's discard
118 Our jazziest president?
122 Where most people live
123 Some ancient mariners
124 "___ elected"
125 Sandy hill
126 Ernst of sound-barrier fame
127 "Solemnly" follower
128 Apply, as pressure
129 LeBron or Leonardo, e.g.

DOWN

1 Catch in a lie, e.g.
2 Site of rods and cones
3 Compliment's converse
4 Feather ___
5 Light lunch
6 Home of the Hopis: abbr.
7 Perfect square
8 Make lace
9 Refuse holder
10 Well below, with "of"
11 Results of key hits
12 Employee of 5 Across
13 Scam
14 Gentleman thief Lupin of fiction
15 BMW rival
16 Name for a jazz revue?
17 Quarterback Tebow
18 Dismiss summarily
24 Tibet's capital
25 Down ___ (Maine)
31 Go on
33 "___ in England ..."
34 Obvious trait of William Tell's son
35 Control substance?
37 Hershey candy
38 Canine complaint
40 *Danse* events
41 City near Provo
42 Door securer
45 Fuse again, in a way
48 Fish made of vitamins?
49 Cornered
50 "Who are ___ guys?"
51 Like jazz movies?
53 Slangy nose
55 Place to surf
57 Wall St. fig.
58 Competition: abbr.
60 30,000 ft., e.g.
63 Order member
66 Set aside
67 Coward's namesakes
70 Not safe
71 Hypothetical questions
72 Words before idea or guess
73 Move south?
76 Kind of computer connection
80 WWI Treasury secretary William
82 Finished the dishes
83 "Frasier" co-star Gilpin
85 Capital near Chernobyl
86 Cruise stop
87 Niagara Falls sound
88 Humorist Bombeck
90 Remaining
94 Seating by the door, on planes
96 Dwindle
99 "... and Jupiter ___ with Mars"
100 "Put your pencils down"
101 "Attention, colonists!"
103 German mark
104 "Burnt" shade
105 Part of 54 Across
109 Rosie's fastener
111 93 Across's home
112 Parks of Montgomery
113 Turn on an axis
114 Lancaster's surf-embrace partner
116 Emeril catchword
117 "Surfin' ___"
119 Result of a vein search?
120 "Friends" actress
121 Church with elders: abbr.

...There always seems to be an a-pun-dance of them

NOTE: *Puns kind of accumulate around my house, so I have to clear them out every so often.*

ACROSS

1 Ballet or film, e.g.
8 Barker on a case
12 Literally, "same name"
19 Good students
21 Good name for a dentist?
22 Like some screenplays
23 What even Paris's father became when Helen of Troy was kidnapped?
25 Wide lace collars named after Charlemagne's mom
26 Take a ___ at
27 Be the master of
28 Place to pick lox
29 Sign on an ice cream shop?
38 Recycling receptacle
41 Prepare for takeoff
42 Does a bank job
43 8 Down drink
44 Harbinger
46 Bible verb
48 Dinero for Diego
49 Hank Williams Jr. tune, "She ___"
50 Comment to a "Star Wars" character after getting him out of a jam?
55 Chess ploy, for short
56 Fast fish
57 With 3 Down, a toaster treat
58 Sharp feller?
59 Word on a coin
60 Unladylike laugh
61 With 70 Across, what Nostradamus always said during roll call (to the constant irritation of his teachers)?
65 Maxim
66 Spot en el mar
68 Mountain lake
69 The B&O et al.
70 See 61 Across
73 Take ___ from one's book
76 Caught in ___
77 Pressure opener
78 Clothes dryer?
79 Current measurer
81 Grasp
82 What goes on in Sue's books?
86 Lake rental
88 Dance of the 1960s
89 Luggage IDs
90 Covers some ground?
91 Neil's slob
92 Peach and cherry, e.g.
93 Puck sells them
95 Butterfly catcher
96 Vehicle of choice for transporting suspects?
102 Depilatory brand
103 Botanical balm
104 Sporty import
107 Naked exemplar
111 "I'm not a bad duck; I'm just ___"
116 Neatened up
117 Christiania, today
118 Like some knives
119 Part of ESP
120 Philly NPR station that produces "Fresh Air"
121 Church dignitary

DOWN

1 It's below Tenn.
2 Weight room units
3 See 57 Across
4 Man with a mission?
5 Via wagering
6 "Shiny Happy People" band
7 Dash of seasoning?
8 Lunchbox staple
9 Diaphanous
10 Little jerk
11 Optional rte.
12 Half a writ
13 Newbery Medal winner Scott
14 Musical stroller?
15 Choose
16 Highest
17 House approval
18 Rx writers
20 Guess
24 Fill-in
28 Urbane
30 "Be More Cynical" comic
31 Semester testers
32 Long haul
33 Hydrant hookup
34 Word in an ABBA musical
35 Weightlessness, to first-timers
36 Striker's item
37 One way to stand
38 "Ben-Hur" co-star Stephen et al.
39 "So why on earth should ___?" (line from "A Hard Day's Night")
40 Pavlov and Alzheimer's thing, generally
45 Zero evidence
47 Overthrow
48 Cartoon skunk
51 Byron poem, "When ___ Parted"
52 Defense org.
53 The yoke's on them
54 Alan's Fed successor
59 Wall-to-wall coverage
62 Unemotional
63 "An intellectual ___! The mind boggles!" (line from 1951's "The Thing from Another World")
64 Disney dog, the ___
66 Llama herder of old
67 Less ventilated
70 On ___ (under tight control)
71 Nasser was its pres.
72 Vampire feature
74 Glittery rock
75 Bond villain's first name
76 High-class tie
79 Trade talk
80 Reluctant reply
82 Plane-exiting cry
83 Prehist. predator
84 Unseat
85 Two-edged swords
87 Stumblebum
92 Sean's persona after Puff Daddy
94 "Now I'm not ___"
97 Less frequent
98 Stage a comeback
99 Brass, for one
100 ___ double-take
101 Like Fran Drescher's voice
105 "___ boy!"
106 V8 juice ingredient
107 Low-ranking USN types
108 "We ___ family ..."
109 That way, once
110 AL team, on scoreboards
111 Do a job that's paid by the yard
112 Eruption fallout
113 Fife, for one: abbr.
114 Prof. Tolkien
115 34th U.S. pres.

ACROSS

1 Innovative comic of 1950s TV
7 "Do you mind?"
11 Big Ben sound
15 Beehive, e.g.
19 "Sister Ree," really
20 Red river?
21 Hawaiian cookout
22 Side with fried catfish, maybe
23 Comic actor who's a serious banjo player
24 *It's not a giant reptile*
26 Worms, sometimes
27 *It's not German for "long-playing records"*
29 Naive
30 Primeval void
31 Author Segal
33 Is full of
34 They might stick out
36 Actor Homolka
40 Shipping inquiry
42 *It's not an obsession with police stun guns*
46 *He's not "the Father of Electricity"*
48 Stallone role
50 Alcatraz, for one
51 "And while ___ it ..."
52 Pretty good
54 Sighed line
56 "... baked in ___ "
57 Casual wear
59 Aurora's counterpart
60 *It's not some guy's name*
62 "The Godfather" composer
64 Sighed line
66 Bonnie's portrayer
67 Spoil
68 Clad like a grad
71 *It doesn't mean "fish of the day"*
74 The Duke, in filmdom
76 "Where am ___ go?"
77 Greek H's
79 Computes columns
80 Decides
82 *It doesn't mean "subtracted"*
85 Mauna ___
87 Bone-related
91 Passable
92 -algia or -ology intro
93 Ceremonial burner
95 Hankering
96 Go by
98 Significant
100 *They're not doggie snacks*
102 *It's not a type of ore*
104 Behind bars
106 Accomplishments
107 Royal in a sari
108 Wile E. Coyote purchase
109 Battery terminal
111 Pounce, bird-style
114 Coastal cataclysm
117 *It's not French for "husband-to-be"*
122 Honolulu's home
123 *It's not a fraction of a penny*
125 Radiator protector
126 Icicle former
127 Bondsman's offering
128 Cousin of adios
129 Virgil's hero
130 "Famous" cookie man
131 "I'm in" indicator
132 Calif. campus 16 mi. N of Tijuana
133 Mystical Arizona town

DOWN

1 "___ Sutra"
2 Unwritten, as a contract
3 Win, place, or show, e.g.
4 Aleutian island
5 Foolish fancy
6 Less likely to lose it
7 Jet level: abbr.
8 "Serves you right!"
9 "... ___ after"
10 Newspaper info box
11 B.B. King's genre
12 Communally owned
13 Mid-Atlantic state?
14 The Theatre Cat in "Cats"
15 Atkins Diet fave
16 "No problemo"
17 Name or flower
18 Trans ___
25 Word after fire or snooze
28 Part of 108 Across
30 Parts of shirts or sofas
32 Minotaur's home
35 "To repeat ..."
36 Exiled Roman poet
37 Vague amount
38 The Kennedys, e.g.
39 Duds
41 Friend's apartment, maybe
42 "L'chaim"
43 Table linen
44 Cast ___ (hard to change)
45 Carol start
47 Research sch.
49 Scrooge's word
53 Male pig
55 1836 battle site
58 Art class subject
60 Street vendors
61 Colorful amphibians
63 ___ in point
65 Dr.-related
68 Dishwasher, at times
69 Lawrence portrayer
70 Dwarf-tree art
72 Take for granted
73 "The Heat ___ "
75 Perceptive
78 Find on the dial
81 Perspiration point
83 ABBA et al.
84 Reliever's stat
86 John who played Gomez
88 Lake S of Detroit
89 Like some beef
90 A smaller amount
93 Gets in touch with
94 Actor Flynn
97 Piece of cake
99 Spirit, in Islamic myth
101 To ___ (somewhat)
103 "Ecce Homo" painter
105 Sullies
108 Veil material
110 "Le Viol" painter
111 Teetotaler's order
112 Toasty
113 Kent State's state
115 Narrow opening
116 Samoa studier Margaret
118 Melon leftover
119 Spread's old name
120 "The Good Earth" heroine
121 Southwestern flattop
123 Wall St. degree
124 Sorority letter

24 | Eat, Drink, and Be Merry

..."Be wary" would be more like it*

ACROSS

1 Bug's warning?
5 Dues payer: abbr.
8 Frazzled mgr.'s hire
12 "Enigma Variations" composer
17 State with conviction
18 Art rock group, Procol ___
20 Out of sorts
21 "Cheers" waitress
22 **Holiday verse, Part 1**
25 Cineplex theater name
26 **Verse, Part 2**
28 In___ation
29 Improvement
32 Cancel
33 Old Testament Bible book
35 Jalopy
36 **Verse, Part 3**
41 Part of 29 Down, literally
42 Potter's purchase
44 "Literacy ... ___" (Bill Clinton)
45 Truth-in-advertising org.
48 Meth ending
49 Chilean child
51 Viva ___ (orally)
52 Green alert?
53 **Verse, Part 4**
58 Post-flood resting spot
60 Snow melter
61 One way to pack tuna
62 Holiday wood
64 Heavyweight fight?
66 **Verse, Part 5**
69 Zola novel
70 Warring ___
74 Not slow
76 Taunting boxer
78 Mini hooters
79 **Verse, Part 6**
84 Alfred E. Neuman feature
85 Abel's brother
86 Extension ___
87 The race car circuit?
89 Workout joint
90 "Must be ___ room temperature"
94 Puppy bites
96 Santa ___ CA
97 **Verse, Part 7**
100 Singer Lauper
102 Star search trio?
104 Part of m.p.g.
105 Thingamajig
106 Calla lily, e.g.
107 **Verse, Part 8**
113 Campaign button site
115 **End of the holiday verse**
119 Unfeeling
120 "I'm ___ your tricks!"
121 Pointed
122 Heart problem?
123 Skater Sonja
124 Tending to snoop
125 Homer's chipper neighbor
126 Santa's team, e.g.

DOWN

1 Scrooge remark
2 The night before Christmas
3 How a ballad might end?
4 Already sliced
5 Hawaiian isle
6 Takes a wrong exit, e.g.
7 "___ touch!"
8 A first-grade recitation
9 Large amount
10 Ganges garb
11 1998 Denzel Washington-Bruce Willis thriller
12 Friendly introduction?
13 Sonny boy
14 North Carolina city
15 Sing-___
16 Tirades
18 Trumpet, e.g.
19 Diva's warmup syllables
23 Green toon voiced by Mike Myers
24 Largest of the Cyclades
27 "Angels we have heard on ___"
29 Where Kareem was still Lew
30 Plug projection
31 Stun guns
34 Do-it-yourself buy
36 Letter or syllable omission
37 Ex-U.N. chief Kofi
38 Sitarist Shankar
39 Cupid's counterpart
40 French regime of WWII
43 It turned away Mary and Joseph
46 Eschew humility
47 Plays the ponies
50 ___ about (approximately)
52 A piece of "Deck the Halls"
54 "Emma" author
55 Igloo dweller
56 Day, in Durango
57 Coquette
58 In the style of
59 Of the kidneys
63 Eda LeShan book, "It's Better To Be Over the Hill Than ___"
65 Dec. and Jan.
67 Lumbering tool
68 Big, big story
70 Literary circumnavigator
71 Wrong
72 Scales, as Santa's knee
73 Bart or Brenda
75 Ex-Turkish leader Ismet
77 Christmas, for one
80 Hurried
81 "The King ___"
82 Econ. indicator
83 Dominique of "The Conformist"
85 Puts trust in
88 Taken care of, as a debt
90 Relative of "abbr."
91 Olympic divers point them
92 Colorado resort
93 Drug-approval admin.
95 'Move over'
98 Certain Red Sea neighbors
99 Actor Josh
101 "___ me at hello"
102 Eagles guitarist Joe
103 Spitting bullets
105 Like red and green hair
108 Cry of dismay
109 Woks, e.g.
110 Ocean marker
111 "The ___ of the Ancient Mariner"
112 ___ out a win
114 Heavy-duty cleaner
116 Winter build-up
117 That girl
118 That girl

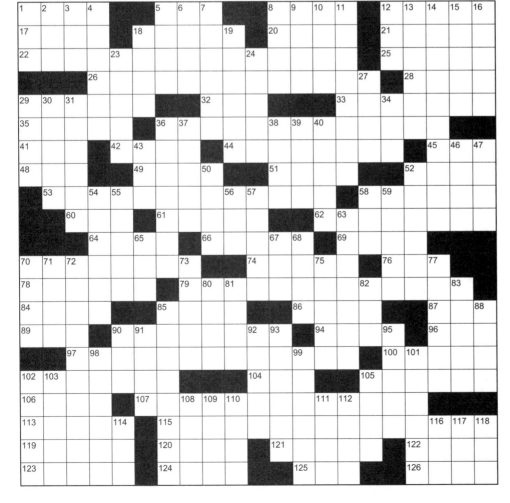

25 | Eat, Drink, and Be Murray

...A stroll down mem-Murray lane

ACROSS

1 His humor is very Kaplanesque
5 Part of a roadie's load
8 "Judge not, lest ___ judged"
12 Nudge (into action)
16 Edison aide-turned-rival
17 Refreshing drinks, or a 1967 film spoof about the music biz (with "The")
19 Cry on the street
20 MURRAY
23 Grazer's sound
24 At any time, to Keats
25 Address ending
26 Gaston's glassful, perhaps
27 "Kiss Me" miss
29 MURRAY
35 Name fit for a king
36 Steer clear of
37 Car builders' org.
38 Location
39 Old, but new again
41 Wife of Zeus
42 Friday, for ex.
43 Bartlett's item
45 The Red or the White
46 MURRAY
53 W.C. Fields exclamation
54 Writer Hamill
55 Glottis opening
56 ___ paper
58 Free of debt, as a business
61 Rampage
62 Edicts
64 Dove's sound
65 One with a policy
66 MURRAY
68 Tequila source
70 Greek letter
71 Gone by
73 Meal for a moth
74 Magoo types
75 Sonar sound
77 Org. with a complex code
78 Part-man creature
79 Cover evenly
80 MURRAY
86 Bristol bottleful
87 Gridiron features, ___ marks
88 Young ___
89 High school subj.
91 Neutral vowel sound
94 Chief Ouray's people
96 Toward the tail
97 Classic, oft-filmed German novel, "___ Briest" (anagram of 72 Down)
98 Detective story pioneer
99 MURRAY
105 "I think somebody needs ___"
107 ___ good deed
108 Surfacing stuff
109 Traffic maneuver: slang
110 The great leveler
111 MURRAY?
117 Lowood orphan of fiction
118 Fills drink orders
119 Did nothing
120 Snorkeler's heaven
121 Sp. miss
122 Prophet's conclusion?
123 Peer of Agatha

DOWN

1 Be in the rotation
2 Mary Kay's last name
3 More like a clear sky
4 Word with dog or lop
5 Oh, in Cologne
6 Dairy denizen, cutely
7 Words before gold or tea
8 "Hey!" follower
9 Like B. Disraeli
10 Command
11 Home with grounds
12 Org. in a class by itself?
13 Stack up (against)
14 Rural conveyance
15 Loser of a sort
16 Windpipe
18 Ovine youngster
20 Humble
21 ___ iron
22 Pat and Mike, e.g.
28 Outer opening?
30 Endlessly
31 Defense org.
32 Water meter data
33 Presumptuous letter starter
34 Math exer.
40 Theater sign
42 Whack
43 Song of praise
44 Doors
45 "M*A*S*H" co-star
47 Odist's Muse
48 Forget being frugal
49 Sam of "Jurassic Park"
50 Friend of Ruby and Beryl?
51 Newscast closer
52 Took the Toyota
57 Tavern in "The Simpsons"
58 Org. with 44 million members
59 KLM's predecessors?
60 Hotelier Helmsley
61 U.S. oil hub
62 "Brigadoon" heroine (played in the film by Cyd Charisse)
63 Doctor's order
66 Toward the nose
67 Tree branch
69 Turn in
72 Mayberry deputy
74 "... gathers no ___"
76 Exhibit beaver behavior
78 Split second
79 Part-man creature
81 Patron saint of Norway
82 Big bird
83 Bungle
84 Bride
85 "What's ___ about that?"
90 Requests to Santa
91 Hydrotherapy haven
92 Talk it over
93 Court announcement
94 Depth-charge targets
95 Parcel inquiry
96 Heart outlets
100 USN VIP
101 Twenty dispensers
102 "We'll see"
103 Reagan attorney general Ed
104 Per annum
106 French Santa, ___ Noel
112 Dict. datum
113 Canadian prov.
114 Govt. product-tester
115 Murphy-Nolte film, "48 ___"
116 Cardinals, on scoreboards

ACROSS

1 He's hooked
5 Signs of disuse
9 Wild guess
13 Palindromic emperor
17 Compact Apple
18 Clog's cousin
19 Word sung by Yalies
20 See 30 Across
21 Old CBS drama (hair)
24 Scoot down a chute
25 Reacts to pain, perhaps
26 Set foot (on)
27 Big Daddy portrayer
29 Good name for a computer instructor?
30 With 20 Across, just for kicks
31 Spine part (skin)
34 Church invitation (hair)
38 Actress who played TV's Lois Lane opposite George Reeves, ___ Neill
39 PAC of docs
40 Test subject
41 "So there!"
42 Aleutian island
44 Baby birds?
47 Soccer player's driver
48 Business without borders (skin)
52 Atlantic foodfish

56 Party centerpiece
57 Cry of mock innocence
58 Film cut
59 Peaceful
60 Epicenters
61 Be in a bee
63 Aliens, briefly
64 Coach's football team, on "Coach" (skin)
68 Many a time
71 ___ against time
72 Molls and dolls
73 Tax nonfiler, perhaps
77 Hammer's end
79 Malt addition
80 Corn-row site
81 Impulse activators
82 Japanese fish dish (skin)
86 Photog's original
87 Rack contents
88 Display-case sparklers
89 Hop-o'-my-thumb
91 Shania Twain tune, "The Woman ___"
92 Fireball from Federer
93 18 Across, e.g.
95 Truly troubled (hair or skin)
97 Letdown (skin)
102 Supportive shout
103 Pale wood
104 Shipped
105 Scintilla

106 Championships
110 Bankrupt
112 Creepy crop in "Invasion of the Body Snatchers" (hair)
115 Cornell of Cornell University fame
116 Name that means "born again"
117 Honeys
118 It might have a twist
119 Air for a pair
120 Program part
121 Nobel Prize subj.
122 Starchy fare

DOWN

1 In the company of
2 Melville novel
3 Brother of Fidel
4 "Cowboy in the city" series
5 Loads (of lucre)
6 Slacken
7 Ken?
8 MVP of Super Bowl I
9 Homer has one
10 *Donner*, in English
11 Parking garage's first floor, often
12 Cotton machine
13 Bird that can rotate its head 270 degrees
14 Hitchhike

15 Tony, for one
16 Last of a series
18 Heavenly being
19 Limp cause, perhaps
22 House layers
23 Rejections
28 Denial, for one?
31 Wonka's creator
32 The good earth?
33 Act big?
34 Crystal impression
35 School for Jules
36 Microwave feature
37 Explosive emotion
42 Sliding-bead adders
43 Preparing to shoot
44 Frying pan
45 Work up a sweater
46 Platoon leaders: abbr.
49 Carol start
50 Oscars org.
51 "Walkabout" director Nicolas
53 Montgomery of jazz
54 Ancient Andean
55 Derived from iron
60 Aspect
61 1965 march site
62 Dolly's last name in "Hello, Dolly!"
65 From Boston to Rome
66 Hart and Larson
67 4 Down's first name
68 Sulzberger in-law
69 Ruckus
70 Aunt of Nicolas Cage
74 "Beats me," slangily
75 Varnish resin
76 Star in Orion, or one of Ben-Hur's chariot horses
78 Benign witchcraft
80 Rat-race rarity
81 Channel buildup
83 Truck-backing-up alerts
84 Ghostbuster played by Harold Ramis
85 Reeve role
90 Avenging spirits, with "the"
91 "Suits me!"
93 14-liner
94 ___ out of the park
95 Shortly, briefly
96 John Galt's creator
97 Had the chutzpah
98 Subaru alternative
99 Squints (at)
100 Herd word
101 Practice piece
106 Adder's-tongue, for example
107 Actress Albright
108 Esau's land
109 Heathrow sights, once
111 Writer Hentoff
113 Theater company, briefly
114 ___ Paulo

27 | A Bunch of Two-Timing Name-Droppers   ...What am I missing here?

NOTE: *The letters in parentheses are the letters that have been dropped from the original name.*

ACROSS

1 Muscular misfire
6 Snacker's bagful
11 Some scores
14 Hellenic H
17 Actress Berger
18 Kin of "me too!"
19 Loop of wire, e.g.
20 Little taste of whisky
21 Park bird that thinks it's a duck? (L D)
23 Not the most popular job at a hydroelectric plant? (A L)
25 "Give ___ chance"
26 Puzo's Tessio
27 Bundles in a field
28 New bill of 2002
29 Temptations classic
32 Pal of Freddy Flamingo? (Z T)
35 Darin's Sandra
36 Swallowed the bait?
37 Forms of dress
38 Secret, as a message
39 Highly irritatin' article? (F R)
42 Gillette razor
43 "Wait ___ Dark"
44 Cigarette-ad word
45 When wives go out? (G K)
51 Menu choice at an Indian restaurant? (V I)
55 Eggs
56 Overthrowing first, e.g.
57 Tea total?
58 Wolves can't help doing it
61 In the manner of
62 Chest protectors
65 Nickname for a motorcycle that runs on garbage? (E L)
69 "Dear me"
70 Lovelace of computer lore
71 Sunday talks
72 Attys.' org
74 Vaccine pioneer's first name
77 With 95 Down, a testing site
78 Not a bad score, perhaps? (T W)
84 Emergency manuals? (B R)
87 ___ Jima
88 Glittering topper
90 Shake hands with
91 Private eye who retrieves deadbeats? (I L)
95 Really excited, in street slang
97 Black Cadillac, often
99 A, *en français*
100 Very old: abbr.
101 Colorfully clad Spanish cousin of Fats? (C G)
103 "___ for the weary"
105 Sentry's cry
106 Victory cry
107 Le Duc ___
110 Fox News rival
111 Answer to "What do you do, Ms. Midler?" (K B)
113 European actress who became an American actor? (M N)
118 Record of events
119 Fluffy scarves
120 Sound
121 Flavorful dressing
122 Stiff-board insert
123 Navy rank: abbr.
124 Take by force
125 Heir to a throne

DOWN

1 Walk this way?: abbr.
2 Shooter insert
3 Farm worker?
4 Shrek's creator William
5 A president might impose it
6 Lab series?
7 Monopolizes
8 Theory, e.g.
9 Fast Eddie prop
10 More than a mistake
11 Actress Marisa
12 Studies in detail
13 Org. in the film "Patty Hearst"
14 Stand the test of time
15 Bicycle spoke, e.g.
16 Chef's protector
19 Cellular buildup?
22 The first chapter
23 Challenge
24 Are low, as tires
27 Swiss city
29 Wherewithal
30 Gossip
31 Slow, in music
33 Popular juice drink
34 "Stormy Weather" star
35 Actress Joanne
37 Prepare (for action)
40 Highland attire
41 Arg. neighbor
42 1938 film, "___ at Oxford"
46 "Which is longer, ___?" (optical illusion query)
47 507
48 Overcast
49 Ian or Celeste
50 Food holder
52 Morse morsels
53 Designer Gucci
54 Panetta and Trotsky
59 Celtic language
60 Equipment
62 Mexican peninsula
63 It might be jewel-encrusted
64 Cause of misery
66 Spartan serf
67 Switch addition
68 Siberian city
69 Feats of illusion
73 Lingering anger
75 Secret targets?
76 Hero's horse
79 Workbench clamp
80 Fluffy grazer
81 Zero laughs
82 A few laughs
83 Nottingham's river
85 Regard with contempt, slangily
86 Done in
89 Circle section
92 Piers Anthony novel (or a Cockney's bugle)
93 Traveling show for GIs
94 Tennyson's Arden
95 See 77 Across
96 Sweet Spanish wine
97 Elias and Gordie
98 "Commander," in Arabic
101 Eagles' city: abbr.
102 Artist Edgar
104 Early computer
108 Brutish Mr. of fiction
109 Psych finish
112 "How can ___ sure?"
113 Lacking training
114 Simple bed
115 Serious traffic violation
116 ___-tourism
117 Stimpy's pal

ACROSS

1 Archer's asset
4 Revolutionary Emiliano
10 Restless desire
14 Hand-held organizers, briefly
18 Colorful carp
19 Captivate
20 "Godzilla" studio, 1954
21 Yummy filling
22 Enthusiast's opinion of a card game?
25 Not so green
26 Stuffy-sounding
27 Like Austen, for ex.
28 Telegram punctuator
29 Essayist and novelist Susan
30 Three in ___
32 With 40 Across, what the expert cardplayer was?
35 Mollify
38 1973 court alias
39 Call to mind
40 See 32 Across
42 German border river
43 Ed's mouse pal Gigio
47 Major leaguer
48 Shepherd's concern
49 Yul Brynner film about cardplayers?
51 Complete
54 Complete a street
55 Muffin ingredient
56 Follow
57 Sprat's diet restriction
59 Two threes, for one
60 Monokini's lack
62 Ear prefix
63 Card lecturer's response to a newbie?
69 Pipe shape
70 Part of a chorus line?
71 Groucho in "Duck Soup"
72 Suggests strongly
73 Hansen who hosted NPR's "Weekend Edition"
75 By and by
76 Engine part
77 Cow catcher
81 Cardplaying capital of Florida?
84 Paddock papas
86 Cruiser occupant
87 Cherry discard
88 Apartment-name word
89 Cardplaying singer?
92 Cornered
94 Inflation meas.
95 Very hot
96 Really aggressive card game?
101 Zip, to 4 Across
102 Give a pep talk to
103 Spanish stewpot
104 Golfer's concern
107 "Beetle Bailey" character
110 Light emitter
111 Shakespeare's cardplaying duo?
114 Laura of "ER"
115 "Aha!"
116 Expiator
117 Sean Lennon's mom
118 A long time
119 Charlie Chan's creator, Earl ___ Biggers
120 Put a new label on
121 Political fig.

DOWN

1 Analogous
2 Teensy bit
3 Fail to score, perhaps
4 Gung-ho
5 Dancer Miller
6 Canapé topper
7 To ___ (unanimously)
8 Neighbor of Fiji
9 Cultural hang-ups?
10 "___ pits!"
11 From head ___
12 Contributed
13 Ad follower
14 Einstein's U.S. home
15 Profundity
16 "… but a Manwich is ___"
17 Suit material
21 Swindler
23 Language of Iran
24 Tycoon John Jacob
29 Bit of laughter
31 WWII auxiliaries
33 Low card
34 Currier's colleague
35 Dr. J's do, once
36 Ethan Hawke-Uma Thurman film
37 Book boo-boos
40 Choose
41 Knack for music
42 Leigh's 1939 Oscar role
44 "___ thought"
45 Cartoon canine
46 "___ a Grecian Urn"
49 Formal orders
50 Underhanded sort
52 "Pick a card, ___ card"
53 Inventory taker?
55 Place for boats
58 Stoat's coat
59 A ___ the back
60 ___ python
61 Gas pump abbr.
63 Puppy protests
64 "Silas Marner" author
65 Quench
66 Cautionary list
67 Ice cream buys
68 Bag-screening agcy.
74 Roundworms
75 Randy Newman tune, "There's a Party ___"
76 Valerie Plame's ex-employer
78 Possible outcomes
79 Some people break into it
80 Photo ___
82 Morocco's capital
83 Asian sea
84 Improv piece
85 Karen's ex on "Will & Grace"
89 Nozzle option
90 Wipeout?
91 "Burr" author
93 They keep things rolling
94 Less agitated
96 Radio and TV, for example
97 Slangy firing
98 French wine valley
99 Burt's Oscar role
100 Election selection
105 Zero ___
106 1954 East Coast hurricane
108 Barry or Rayburn
109 Princely prep school
111 Unburden
112 Galley prop
113 Atticus Finch's boy

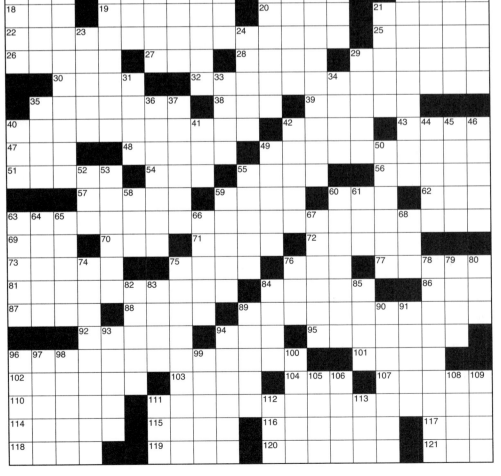

29 Basket of Goodies

...Coloring them is optional

ACROSS

1 Exercise your canines
6 Tourmaline, e.g.
9 Shortened, as a dict.
12 Armored contestant
14 Paris suburb
15 Euclid's forte: abbr.
17 Swiss composer (1892-1955)
19 Be-all's partner
22 Hits guru Casey
24 "___ put all your eggs ..."
25 Eggs-and-bacon establishment, perhaps
27 Showman's first name
28 Actress Samantha of "The Collector"
31 "Really?"
33 With great passion
34 "Juiced" author
36 1945 college comedy, "Here Come the ___"
37 "___ man answers ..."
39 Dock workers' org. (or backwards, a boxer)
40 I, she, it, or you, for example: abbr.
41 Bunny's feet
42 Actor Herbert of "Pink Panther" fame
43 Diarist Anaïs
44 Stylish Schiaparelli
47 One way to pay
49 Legendary flagmaker
51 Ventura Fwy. speeder stopper
52 Ness, for one
53 Actress Peeples or Vardalos
54 Requiring string, as some decorations
56 Sunny ___ (egg preference)
59 Easter month, in Paris
61 Miss your exit, e.g.
63 Test-question choice
64 The "I" of LASIK
65 Hot or cold drink
66 Holiday event, with 14 Down
70 To ___ for
71 Clown Kelly
73 Type of fish, or a TV host missing her middle
74 PJs-wearing CEO
75 Poor as ___
77 Pay one's ___ society
78 Taboos
80 Summer clock change: abbr.
82 Check on the apartment?
83 Rel. of kid gloves
84 Condé ___
86 Eruption action
88 Approximately
89 3M game, "Oh-Wah-___"
90 For each
91 "The wolf ___ the door"
92 Timber wolf
94 Common joiner
95 Ceremony capper
96 "Waiting for Lefty" playwright
97 Waffle-lover's cry, in commercials
101 Model
103 Actress Henner
105 Plane hdg.
106 Unprecedented time
107 Anagram of "Easter egg"
109 Actor Baldwin
112 Inclines
114 Merchant ship
115 He has a two-second cameo in 2003's "The Rundown"
119 Evening, in Evian
120 Bring home the bacon
121 Oil units
122 Touch-Tone 6
123 "We ___ family ..."
124 Does a meter job

DOWN

1 An Al
2 Connecticut resident's nickname
3 Baseball-bat wood
4 Early Beatle Sutcliffe
5 Roundup bunch
6 Shorthand pioneer, or Mrs. Muir's ghostly captain
7 Chooses
8 Breckinridge and Hess
9 Author-critic James
10 English jurist-philosopher Jeremy (1748-1832)
11 Show that throws a lot of people
12 Argo guy
13 Greek letter
14 See 66 Across
16 German philosopher (1889-1976)
18 Poached eggs ___
20 They fought a war over which end of an egg to break
21 ___ egg (bomb)
22 Col. Sanders' place
23 In the style of
26 Thwarts, as a theft
29 Flip ___
30 Football's Lott and music's Milsap
32 Prod. endorsements?
35 Turkish horseman (anagram of A SHIP)
36 One for the books?
38 Dig discovery
44 Thrilled
45 Anagram of DENVER OMELET
46 GESG?
48 Egg containers
49 No cakewalk
50 Film short's length, perhaps
51 Today's platters
55 Work unit
57 1985 film, "To Live and Die ___"
58 ___ Vallarta
60 Riga resident, variantly
62 Transplant, in a way
67 Did penance
68 Was gooey, like an undercooked egg
69 Pediophobia, the fear ___
72 Useful Latin abbr.
76 Water-carrier in Disney's "Sorcerer's Apprentice"
79 Egg flipper
81 Breakfast order
85 Egg-frying emanation
87 Myers and McHenry: abbr.
89 Gorbachev's wife
90 Enters en masse
91 Dada, the ex-dictator
93 Like a cowboy's walk, maybe
96 Vehicle of mine?
98 Quite a spell
99 Encourage
100 Clip-___
102 Get ___ for the night
104 In a quandary
108 Greek snack
110 Tarzan's creator: inits.
111 Drug official
113 Snakes in lakes
116 Old Germanic empire: abbr.
117 Before, old-style
118 One of FDR's agencies

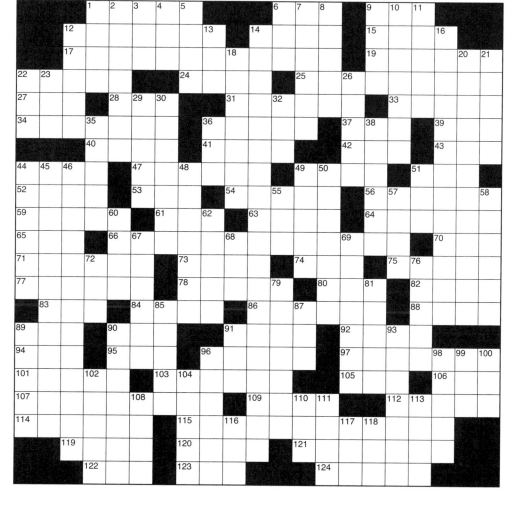

ACROSS

1 Work crew
6 Eva's other sister
11 Food additive
14 Chat room venue
17 Slangy smoke
18 Deodorant type
19 Where Martin Luther King Jr. is buried
21 "Burke's Law" producer
23 Ones with a material interest?
24 Fvll-deck total
25 Stand in
26 Cop show catchphrase
28 "Tighten Up" singer of '68
33 3, in Turin
34 Word before "hour," often
35 Be over
36 Name in Lucas lore
38 Classic Stones album of '66
43 Council
46 Accepted, as money owed: abbr.
48 Norton namesakes
49 Vote against
50 Part of a talking-horse song
56 Ready to eat
57 "Rubbish"
58 Like Santa's suit on Dec. 26
59 Beginning
60 Trap, in a way
61 Singer Pinza
63 Sweet finish?
64 Beatles-era Brits
65 Arid area
66 Actress who was Miss Miami of 1969
71 Sells at inflated prices
73 Bupkis, in Bogota
74 Sound: abbr.
75 Jennifer married him
78 Breakthrough word in "The Miracle Worker"
79 Heathen
80 Whirling, old-style
82 "___ minute!"
83 Surrounded by
84 "Catch-22" entrepreneur
87 Old Olds auto
88 Family member
89 Close tightly
90 "My Fair Lady" composer
91 Daytime dealmaker, once
95 The Graf ___
97 Hurricane-wary st.
98 Vit. C info
99 Dept.'s cousin
101 "Jeopardy!" host of the '60s
106 "The Silencers" star
110 Actor Gulager
111 Company VIP
112 Disapprove of strongly
113 What this puzzle's theme has, literally?
118 Like some jacks
119 Cruise woe
120 Bridge need
121 Jazz great Montgomery
122 Reagan's space-laser idea: abbr.
123 Affirmatives
124 Sides in an age-old battle

DOWN

1 Word before step or way
2 Donut-shaped
3 "Long ___ ..."
4 $5 bill
5 ___ up (admitted)
6 Tiny particle: abbr.
7 Tie-score word
8 Like smooth, offhand talk
9 ___ ENTER
10 Typical Ed Wood material?
11 Spouse
12 Western action scene
13 Simple planes
14 In due time
15 Other, in Oaxaca
16 ___ Cruces
17 Room in a *casa*
18 Convention flouter
20 Smoke detector
22 Alehouse
27 Indian hemp
29 Superman, e.g.
30 Hyderabad's river
31 Painter Neiman
32 Beloved, to the Bard
37 Plays along with
39 Assay, e.g.
40 County fair offering for kids
41 Hoglike mammal
42 Wolflike mammal
43 Yawner
44 "The Wizard ___"
45 Removal from mothballs
47 One who gives
51 Historic miniseries
52 Mediocre
53 Like Rome
54 Cabinet unit that Albert Fall once ran: abbr.
55 Trap again
56 Recovery prog.
60 Gen. Arnold's nickname
62 Well-___ (drunk)
65 Part of a 45
67 EMT's forte
68 Play plotter
69 He was Smart
70 He gives you prompt attention
71 Buzzing bunch
72 Brief appearance
76 Over again
77 Challenge
79 ___ colada
80 Stage coach Stella
81 City in N France
84 Islam's founder
85 Wine hub
86 Activist Chomsky
88 Pollack and Greenstreet
92 Baseball deal
93 Queen or president: abbr.
94 Repetitive listing
96 Ohio Art's ___-Sketch
97 Mistakes
100 Aqua ___ (strong liquor)
102 Andy Capp's wife
103 "As if ___!"
104 Tree houses
105 Kid's cry
106 Finished
107 Chemical endings
108 "The King ___"
109 French word whose last two letters are what it means in English
112 Farm critter
114 Take off the shelf
115 These, in Paris
116 Runner Sebastian
117 Detergent sponsor of many old TV shows

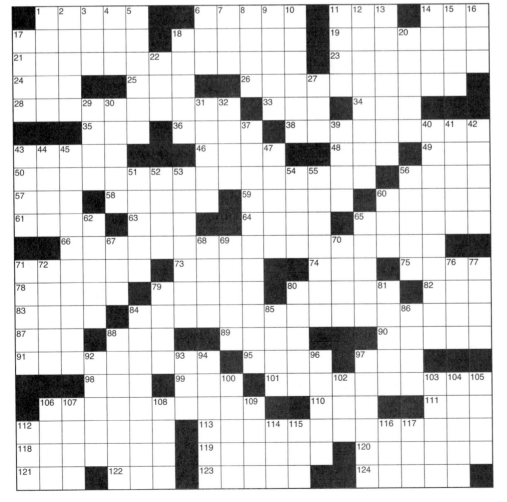

ACROSS

1 Ozawa contemporary
6 Workout pain
11 Romance novelist Roberts
15 IBM release of 1984
19 Taxco ta-ta
20 They might be mirages
21 Overcast sky, to some
22 Oliver Sacks best-seller, "The Man Who Mistook His Wife for ___"
23 "Let's see … this is the tennis player's kid …"
25 "This is the mechanic's kid …"
27 Shortened holiday?
28 Guns, to Guillermo
29 Information
30 "Antony and Cleopatra" prop
31 Dash units
33 Hairy as ___
35 Sun blocker
39 "This is the caterer's kid …"
44 Tar over
45 ___ crossroads
46 Number of Psalms, plus I
47 Beethoven's Third
50 Salt Lake City team
51 "This is the soldier's kid …"
56 ___ favor
57 Roadie's loads
58 Colon opening
59 TV remote abbr.
60 Strike ___
62 Witch
65 Williams of "Happy Days"
68 Not-yet-mature eggs
70 It may shock you
73 "This is the Olympic star's kid …"
77 "With it"
78 Type of bridge
80 Betray, in a way
81 Hottie, perhaps
83 Bellicose types
84 Small amount
87 Lively, on a score: abbr.
89 Magazine contents
93 Greek letter
94 "This is the clam digger's kid …"
99 Tent door
100 Everlasting, to Enrico
101 Red or White team
102 One before bi
103 Under-the-ocean
105 "This is the traffic cop's kid …"
110 As a rule
112 Rob, to Rob Roy
113 The ___-i-Noor Diamond
114 TV listing abbr.
115 Hammockbound
118 Taiwanese island
120 Millennium, to Miss Marple
124 "This is the Italian-restaurant owner's kid …"
127 "This is the crossword guy's kid …"
129 Healing plant
130 "What's/happening?" insert
131 How sardines may be packed
132 Some stablemates
133 Old Vegas casino, with "The"
134 Concerning
135 Ziti's cousin
136 Stockpile

DOWN

1 Rufus T. Firefly portrayer
2 Waxed cheese
3 Informal greeting
4 Sleeps fitfully
5 Free ___ bird
6 Skim the clouds
7 Binky and Pinky game
8 "___ ye shall receive"
9 Playground sight
10 Wintertime in the Rockies: abbr.
11 Superstar?
12 Drop
13 Sports update
14 FAQ response
15 "This is the pet-store owner's kid …"
16 "This is the dentist's kid …"
17 It holds the mayo
18 Numbered rd.
24 Fight, colloquially
26 Swiss river
29 Disrepute, to Depardieu
32 Department store founder
34 Wharf extension
36 Irish island group
37 Be in charge of
38 French article
39 Half a spy
40 Word derivation: abbr.
41 Shocked reaction
42 Troubles
43 Pegs used in quoits
48 "How can ___ sure?"
49 Crayola choice
52 Burning issue?
53 Private-jet pioneer
54 Bus starter
55 Less naive
60 Have a longing
61 Thought-provoking gift?
63 Variety show offerings
64 Oakley, for one
66 Mama bear, to Maria
67 Of birth
69 Halloween time: abbr.
70 Ordinal suffix
71 Detergent brand
72 "This is the tailor's kid …"
74 Argue back
75 Author Morrison
76 Step ___ (hurry)
79 "This is the farmer's kid …"
82 Day break
85 September hurricane
86 Stomping grounds: abbr.
88 ___ Helens
90 Windsurfing mecca
91 Flash Gordon foe
92 Ken or Lena
94 Faithful, old style
95 Nose noise
96 Primo
97 Hunt for in the dictionary
98 World's fair
99 Tallahassee sch.
104 Old music notes (or 119 Down, backward)
106 Novelist de Beauvoir
107 "Venus" singer
108 Takes hold
109 Mayberry exclamation
111 "Holy smokes!"
116 Return to slender
117 Host does a weekly segment called "Headlines"
119 Tent event
121 Pound of poetry
122 Spanish version of "Cheers"?
123 1987 Costner role
124 Popular pan spray
125 Billionaire philanthropist Broad
126 Lawyers' league: abbr.
127 Enjoy liqueur, e.g.
128 Emma in "The Avengers" (1998)

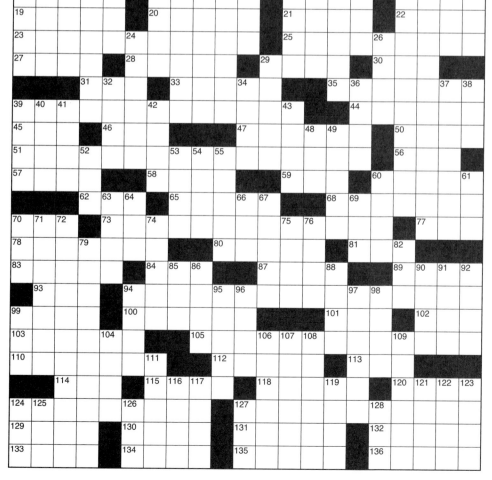

ACROSS

1 With mo, a speed
4 Late-night Carson
8 Stat-heavy channel
12 Each
16 On the ___ vive
17 "___ you just wanna watch TV?"
18 Tag beam
20 Red Cross founder's first name
22 Intro to tech
23 Giving the jumpier pets some exercise?
26 "___ touch!"
28 Early computer
29 Walk-on part?
30 Shots from the foul line: abbr.
32 Islamabad's loc.
33 Six martinis and one big olive?
36 Show approval toward
39 Salty delicacy
40 Showman's first name
41 Wrinkle remover
42 Levi's with an elastic waistband?
44 John of mystery
45 Talk too much
47 Comrade in arms
48 Swiss river
49 Hollywood producer ___ C. Siegel
50 Civilian army
54 What goes on at the Happy Shirt and Skirt Factory?
59 Natural soother
61 One-named Art Deco master
62 Every bit
63 Asian opening
64 What the escape-minded goats were?
71 Welding flash
72 Granola fleck
73 Translate as
74 "West Side Story" director
75 Soda-shop owner's decision after the flyers didn't work?
82 Some chords
83 Gen-___ (boomer's kid)
84 Buckeyes' sch.
85 Bygone autocrat
89 Raises
90 Lifeguard skill
91 With 100 Across, what Carey and Barrymore do at Christmastime?
94 "You're a ___, Alice"
97 Org. founded by the Arab League
98 Tree rescuee
99 1783's Treaty ___
100 See 91 Across
105 ___ out a win
106 Md. neighbor
107 Islands off Ireland
108 Santa's favorite snacks?
109 Smell the coffee, e.g.
112 One way to spice up mashed bananas at the zoo?
116 Cereal brand
117 Loudness units
118 Book after Daniel
119 Hindu goddess that sounds like a dog
120 1941 film, "The Lady ___"
121 Converse competitor
122 Lean and tough
123 Golden ___ (senior)
124 Abbr. seen while taping

DOWN

1 Metric area meas.
2 Outdoor party
3 Coastal disaster
4 Scrolling need
5 Smell ___
6 The "bad" cholesterol
7 Jed or Jethro, e.g.
8 Currents of concern
9 Shrewd, in Italian
10 College maj.
11 Start to con?
12 Allergic reaction
13 Wise Athenian
14 Parter of the waters
15 Like better
19 Gathered strip of fabric
21 Space City player
24 Prepare for burial, as ashes
25 "___ Cop"
27 Hunting cries
31 IRS form datum
33 Starting squad
34 Long past
35 "Not another word!"
36 Suffragist's inits.
37 Tillis of country
38 In ___ (stuck)
43 Mountain Zone team, on scoreboards
44 Irish county
45 Give in
46 Much like
49 Was within popcorn-sharing distance, perhaps
50 Fr. miss
51 Tall-cake features
52 Operating
53 A Cabinet dept.
55 Hang a ___ (head back the other way)
56 Still in the package
57 Even less cheerful
58 Oom-___ band
59 Garfield's middle name
60 Longtime soap star
65 Brewer Adolph
66 Bean warmers?
67 Ordinal suffix
68 It's blown out of proportion
69 Part of MYOB
70 Award-winning Russian violinist David (1908-74)
71 "Lost" network, originally
76 Big name at Notre Dame
77 Climber's goal
78 John McCain, for one
79 "___ lied"
80 "___ at all railroad crossings"
81 Back talk
86 Runner in the raw
87 Sushi bar tuna
88 Where you live: abbr.
90 Grip tightly
91 Time for Tide, maybe
92 Dumas dueler
93 Alfresco
94 Casting need
95 Agenda details
96 "Hey, check it out!"
97 Say grace
98 Picnic container
101 Cleared of leaves
102 Vera Wang creation
103 "... loves me, ___ know"
104 Honshu port
109 Archipelago part
110 Like sports telecasts, often
111 Office-with-a-view type
113 JAX to NYC, e.g.
114 "___ convenient"
115 Fall a little

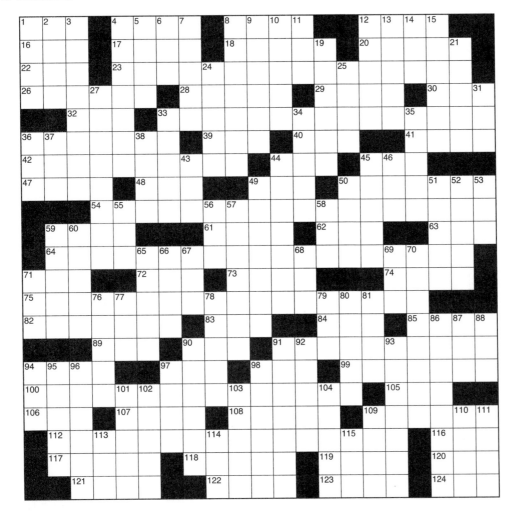

NOTE: *One of the definitions of bath is "bathtub," which makes the word something of a linguistic rarity: bath, tub, and bathtub are all synonyms — or "trinonyms," if you will. After stalking these odd birds for many years I found only ten others — just enough for a puzzle.*

ACROSS

1 "___ to you!"
5 Roughs it, perhaps
10 Rocky projections
15 Uxmal resident
19 Climber's goal
20 In regard to
21 Zodiac sign
22 Page for letters to the editor and such
23 Hat fabric
24 **Holiday critter**
26 Source of pep?
27 Latin 101 word
28 Candle feature
29 NASA acronym
30 It's 53 miles from the U.S.
32 Mr. Whitney
33 **Squealer**
35 Fix, as software
37 **Hotel sight**
39 Right on the note
40 **It's in the can**
42 Basic beliefs
43 Like a paramecium
45 Supermodel Bündchen
47 Sector
50 **Vanguard**
54 Microwaves
58 Ore. neighbor
59 Judge
61 By way of
62 "Fast Food Nation" author Schlosser
65 Sine ___ non
66 Ore. neighbor
67 **Kitchen sub**
70 Swiss canton
71 "Analyze This" star
73 "Sweet Smell of Success" screenwriter
74 Flashers in space
76 Dripping
77 Come before, timewise
79 On Soc. Sec.
80 **Preserve, perhaps**
84 **Entrain, for example**
89 Restricted ___
90 A backer of
91 House, for ex.
92 Malayan boat
93 **Milk lover**
96 Bank or store feature
99 **Entirety**
102 Less of a bear
103 Entertainer Lewis
105 Langston Hughes poem, "Life ___"
106 With 119 and 123 Across, source of this puzzle's theme answers? *
111 In the past
114 Mr. Rubik
115 The Graf ___
116 Who, to Henri
119 See 106 Across
123 See 106 Across
126 Slangy $100 bill
127 Microwave
128 Door sign
129 Ralph of "The Waltons"
130 Camel's back-breaker
131 Tell's partner
132 Good-___
133 Self-evident truth

DOWN

1 Wild adventure
2 Jane's guy, e.g.
3 Giant slugger
4 Ofc. line
5 Place for liquor
6 1985 Kentucky Derby winner, Spend ___
7 Shalhoub's germophobe
8 Groan and bear it?
9 More than just cut, as hair
10 Stop talking
11 Umbrella part
12 "Waterloo" group
13 Future flour
14 Overfill
15 Do the floor
16 Per
17 Bawl out
18 Unscripted stuff
25 One-word WB sitcom
28 Troubles drowner
31 Skating feat
34 Be angry
35 Active one
36 "Faster, faster!"
38 Woman's name
40 Replay effect, briefly
41 Yearning one
44 "___ Pretty"
46 "Blondie" or "Dilbert"
47 Metal in pennies
48 Baltic feeder
49 Blue hue
51 Circumvented
52 "You're ___!"
53 Motley
55 Blue hue
56 Siamese comment
57 Know, to Rousseau
59 Grandparent, perhaps
60 Thrill
63 Store, as ashes
64 Oscars attendee
68 Cuba's ___ Castle
69 Fall bloomer
72 "Don't ___" ("Relax")
75 Visit briefly
77 Left on deck?
78 Verb with *vous*
80 Heist haul
81 Met solo
82 Sometimes they're allowed
83 Tax pro
85 Buckeyes' sch.
86 Intro to drawing, maybe
87 Reddish horse
88 Roy's gal
94 Slangy assent
95 Guiding principle
96 "Bingo!"
97 Road goo
98 1980s Peppard co-star
100 Bishop's hat
101 General ___'s Chicken
103 A Dr., a TV Mr., and others
104 "Do Ya Think ___"
107 Had a few
108 World-weariness
109 "Silas Marner" girl
110 ___-foot oil
111 Trajectories
112 Lady's man
113 It'll stink up the place
116 Liner, briefly
117 Passé preposition
118 Detail
120 Abbr. on Salt Lake City buses
121 "What are you, ___?"
122 Classic-rock group
123 Ball belle
124 Erstwhile carrier
125 Nathan in "The Producers"

* With acknowledgments to the fabulous Firesign Theatre, who coined this term in the 1970s.

ACROSS

1 Monkey's munchie
7 "Faster! Faster!"
11 Misbehaved
17 Mythical dreamboat
18 Traces of the past
20 Ecstasy
21 Singer with a great set of pipes?
23 Out ___ (irritable)
24 *Si* follower
25 Author whose story lines are full of holes?
27 Title anew
29 Chin extension?
30 Oregon's Hood and others: abbr.
31 More, in Monterrey
32 One of two circus supports
34 Type of wrestling
36 Dancer Charisse
37 TV channels 14 and up
40 Guitarist who's not big on snacking?
45 Lack of modesty
48 Philadelphia suburb, ___ Cynwyd
50 Like some massages
51 As a result of wagering
53 No longer on the board
56 Being, to Brutus
57 "___ old cowhand ..."
60 Right now, to an RN
61 Toys for tots
63 People of the Sun
65 Popular Bayer antibiotic
66 1960s activist who's calm at all times?
70 Cybercafe patrons
71 Salad type
72 Break into bits
74 Saint associated with the first oratorios
75 Starting
76 Signals OK
79 Feel sorrow
80 Wood nymphs
82 Monkees hit, "Last ___ Clarksville"
85 Street ___
86 Grizzly, to Guzman
87 Naval officer who likes to shoot a few baskets?
92 Admittance alert: abbr.
93 Craig Ferguson's network
95 Good name for a Russian runner, perhaps
96 Pie nut
98 Wade opponent
99 Wonder
100 Best-liked: abbr.
103 "Adios!"
106 Cabinet member who doesn't buy houses?
111 Start of a Eugene O'Neill play
113 Go long, as a meeting
114 Christmas poet who's kind to convicts?
116 Yom Kippur observers
117 Flip side of the Beatles' "Help!" (1965)
118 Overlooks
119 Cole Porter's "___ We Fools"
120 Galley gear
121 Say yes

DOWN

1 Skycap's cartful
2 Psychiatrist Alfred
3 "Trust ___"
4 Bruckner and Karas
5 Fertilizer material
6 "___ get older ..."
7 Film category
8 Literal or figurative stews
9 Lively dance with a French name
10 N.Y. newspaper name
11 "What ill wind ___ you hither?"
12 Church recess
13 Turbulent
14 Actress who doesn't like owing money for too long?
15 John Dewey book, "___ Experience"
16 It may have locking drawers
18 "Top Hat" studio
19 Additive that once sponsored Richard Petty
20 Russian port on the Don
22 Wheat varieties
26 Bullets
28 Score clock abbr.
33 Kite eater in "Peanuts"
34 Melville subject
35 More repulsive
36 Peas keeper?
37 Above, in Bonn
38 Serious pests
39 Writer who can't help saying nice things?
41 Naval rank: abbr.
42 Emerson efforts
43 1956 crisis site
44 Lithium ___ battery
46 What drivers shift, in Britain
47 Kevin in "A Fish Called Wanda"
49 The Waldorf-___
52 Flu strain
54 Some Ivy Leaguers
55 Busy Bowl game mo.
58 1900
59 Yard-sale caveat
62 Structures resembling 1 Down
64 Coal or pine product
65 Blacken, as a steak
67 Thai tongue
68 Didn't disturb
69 Dashboard abbr.
70 Loosen, as a knot
73 Tie again, as a knot
75 Tempe sch.
77 Abbr. after a Trenton politico's name
78 Metro station
81 Nightclub "spinmeisters"
83 Joplin piece
84 "Be right with ya"
88 Lawn cutters
89 Many a prayer
90 Author Umberto
91 Danglers in delis
94 "Thy will ___"
97 Part of a rolling stone expression
98 Way
99 At the ready
100 "Band of Gold" singer Payne
101 Jouster's covering
102 Opinions or panoramas
104 Ominous loop
105 Bridge pro Charles
106 Stick in one's ___
107 It's hot in here
108 Biol., e.g.
109 Sailor's saint
110 Home of "Headline News"
112 Hornets' home
115 Singer Sumac

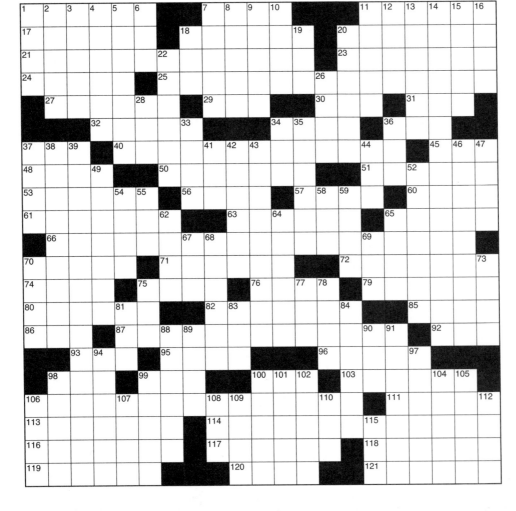

...And now for something completely different

NOTE: *Although I'm the one in the movie* Wordplay *who talks about all the rules that puzzlemakers have to follow, sometimes you just have to take your brain out of its cage and let it run free. So here's a themeless puzzle that breaks two rules — uncrossed letters and two-letter words — and has a grid you don't exactly see every day (not to mention eight interlocking 21-letter entries).*

ACROSS

1 Offerings in tiny type
18 Bill from France
19 Element named after a physicist
20 "That's the way it's gonna be then, eh?"
21 Kin of inc.
22 A and B in D.C., e.g.
24 Rum drink, Cuba ___
25 Freud, to friends?
27 Noted pitier of fools
28 Commuting choice
29 Frets
31 Horner put his thumb in it
32 Blood component
34 Rel. of extra innings
35 Cabbie's query
37 Best Picture of 1984
39 Info-gathering of a sort
40 Legislative bodies
41 Pure no more
42 Watch this?
44 Places
45 Church perch
47 Allude
48 "Little Women" sister
49 Tasty tuber
51 Military address?
52 Elaine's last name on "Seinfeld"
54 Kin of "awesome!"
55 Air mover
56 Let out
58 "Au contraire!"
60 Actress Martha
61 Polite response
62 Spheres to be wary of
63 Lake craft
64 Automaker Maserati
66 Singing series
67 Sweet conclusion
68 Hospital patient's need: abbr.
70 Agrees (with)
71 Change one's locks?
73 Ferrell's fmr. show
74 Concerning
75 ___ a beet
77 Requested, to Snuffy Smith
78 Cowardly Lion's reward
80 Pertaining to
81 Fit for store shelves
83 Second Amendment word
85 Watch-and-learn concept
86 Tit for tat
87 Of an eye part
88 Poet cummings
90 Irritates
91 One of the Cratchits
93 Stops arguing, for example
94 "I just remembered!"
95 A-waste monitor: abbr.
97 B12, for ex.
98 From Jakarta, for example
100 Jane Russell's character in "The Outlaw"
101 Kick ___ fuss
102 Cash drawer
104 Found work
106 Pronto
107 Misfit

DOWN

1 Star power in merchandising
2 Peaceful interlude
3 Shuttlecock's path
4 See 20 Across
5 Pacific divider
6 Hypothetical situation
7 It may be smoked
8 Tap problem
9 Of two minds
10 Desperate
11 Saturn model
12 Dorothy's aunt
13 Famed WWII fighting force
14 Oaxacan OK
15 Ideal finish?
16 Ancient libertine
17 Exercising, etc.
22 Trent Lott's predecessor
23 Father's Day gift
25 More sordid
26 Appeared (on a show)
29 Closet collection
30 Pigpens
32 Makeup mishap
33 Thinking type, in a way
35 London loos
36 Org. in old spy tales
37 Put-on
38 Superagent in "Doonesbury"
43 "Am-scray!"
45 Cartoon pig
46 What thumbs-up signs usually mean
48 Follower of the news?
50 Bishop's hat, to a Brit
52 Yahoos
53 Corporate types, synecdochically
55 Picturesque water scenes
57 Your, among Friends
58 Comedian Louis
59 ___-surfing (googling yourself)
60 Cleaning cloth
65 Longtime variety show host
68 El Al stop
69 Advisory group
71 Editor, at times
72 Deplete, as profits
75 Speed demon
76 Struggles (through)
78 Certain runner
79 Bonet and others
81 California's Big ___
82 Hurricane heading, perh.
83 Debussy's "La ___"
84 Afflict
89 Ex-"ER" star La Salle
91 Filmmaker Jacques
92 Goya subject
94 Iridescent gem
96 Actor Gulager
98 Cardio workout
99 A conjunction
101 R&R provider for GIs
103 Music note
104 One of the appliance giants
105 Derek or Diddley
106 See 20 Across

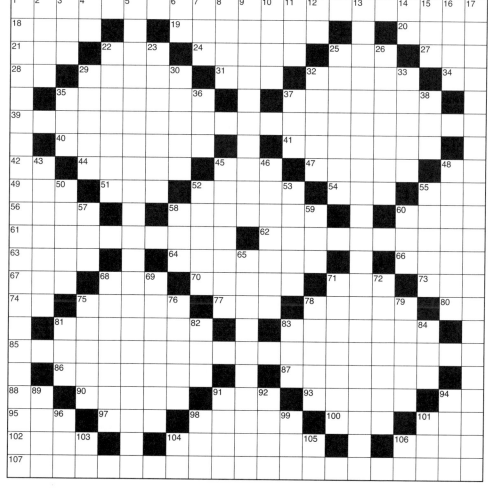

...Kind of a tense situation

ACROSS

1 Poitier role
6 Franklin D.'s mother
10 Sonar sound
14 Popular writers?
18 Microscopic menace
19 Keep or look followers
20 Tom's "Splash" co-star
21 Book about the IRS, "___ Unto Itself"
22 Mailed an exam result?
24 "___ Male War Bride"
25 Opening hour, often
26 Strain, as one's patience
27 Complicated, as a divorce
28 Made a simple fruit preserve?
30 Dusk, to the Bard
31 Medical washing
33 Victor's shout
34 Overlooked a certain wine? [think 1960s TV]
37 Elbow grease
40 "To Kill a Mockingbird" screenwriter
41 Had its last performance
42 Actress Lenska
43 Write (down)
46 Ben Stiller's mom
47 Ran into
48 Chose a chart?
52 Foothold of a sort
54 Branded
55 He played Emile in "South Pacific"
56 Bag content
57 "The results ___"
60 Put away
61 New cars, trips, etc.
63 With 65 Across, looked over a bird?
65 See 63 Across
67 Mother of Joseph
70 Fail to mention
72 Cutting from the payroll
73 Retired plane
76 Sound rebound
77 "The Threepenny Opera" penner
79 Artist's studio
81 Got a pastry chef drunk?
84 Some sports cars
85 Bible preposition
86 Actor Robbins
87 Delhi wrap
88 Pedal-to-the-metal detector?
90 Peter Gunn portrayer Stevens
91 Shale features
93 Stared at Calvin or Robert?
95 "I'm not ___" (Nixon)
98 Sad, to Sartre
100 Big bk.
101 Made a devotee stumble?
104 Actress Verdugo
106 Son-gun insert
109 McCloud's home
110 Atari founder Bushnell
111 Was familiar with the competition?
113 Aleutian island
114 Precise
115 "Wishing won't make ___"
116 Take illegally
117 Breathing: abbr.
118 Unit of force
119 Editing site
120 Apples and pears

DOWN

1 Class struggle?
2 Champagne bucket, e.g.
3 Too thin
4 Crunchy sandwich
5 Cat breed
6 McCartney and Jagger, e.g.
7 Not upright
8 "Fuzzy Wuzzy" poet's first name
9 Chest-beating vegetarian
10 Sioux foe
11 Where Qum is
12 Financial page abbr.
13 Plant with funnel-shaped flowers
14 Stagecoach robber
15 War epic
16 Last words of "Over the Rainbow"
17 Kin of "cool!"
20 Type of illus.
23 Pool unit?
28 Bag handlers
29 "What ___ it is getting old" (the Rolling Stones)
30 Fragrant compound
32 No. 2 types
34 Street card game
35 Asia Minor region
36 Intensify
38 Old Dow floor cleaner
39 Follower of twacks
40 Like lightning
43 Coltrane's thing
44 Role for Ronny
45 Jefferson, briefly
47 Wall art
49 Tonic starter
50 Swedish monetary unit
51 Control
53 Run for the money
58 Spacey
59 Site of ancient Greek games
61 Pub orders
62 Spread unchecked
63 Broadway staple
64 Gumshoe
66 Pfizer product
67 Break
68 63 Down start
69 Certain sci.
71 "___ lies a tale"
73 Locale in Exodus
74 Take hold
75 Joan Crawford's last film
77 The Vamp of silents
78 Cafeteria stack
80 Enticed
82 Bar legally
83 Became overcast
84 Didn't bring home as much bacon
89 Treaty result
90 Resolve
91 Absorbs, as gravy
92 Take ___ value
94 Hawaiian coffee area
95 Rose perfume
96 Jalopy
97 Major melees
99 Dennis Miller commentary
102 Ortho follower
103 Freed from Cleveland
105 Furry Lucas creation
106 Egg
107 The going rate?
108 The Bernese ___
111 Ilsa, to Rick
112 "Equal" starter

…"Here's something I hope you'll really like"

NARRATOR: *Will Bullwinkle be able to extricate himself?*

BULLWINKLE: *I will as soon as I get loose!*

Forthwith, an homage to one of my favorite cartoon shows.

ACROSS

1 Rival of Rival
5 Receive word
9 Baryshnikovs they're not
13 Anthem player at Woodstock
17 "That's an order"
18 Foiler of thieves
19 *With 23 Across, segment narrated by Edward Everett Horton*
21 *Voice of Rocky (and Natasha, and others)*
23 *See 19 Across*
25 Swiss canton
26 Heat, to a hood
28 Make it to the end
29 Pitch hitter?
30 *With 46 Across, Rocky and Bullwinkle's favorite newspaper (aptly enough)*
35 Mental claim
36 San Marino surrounder
38 Crew equipment
39 Hastens
40 Just out
42 Directory datum: abbr.
44 Ryder Cup org.
45 Chapter of history
46 *See 30 Across*
51 Joyce Carol or Warren
54 Govt.-issued ID
56 Healing plants
57 Equine shade
58 *Rocky and Bullwinkle's Minnesota hometown*
62 Took the car
63 It's got the power
64 Man of mystery
65 Flex finish
68 Kipling orphan
69 Oil-can letters
72 *The show's narrator (who later had his own hit series)*
76 Like some grins
77 Formal buy, informally
78 "___ the idea"
79 East or west add-on
80 Together, in music
82 Skilled
84 *The moon men in the "metal-munching mice" episode*
91 Oscar-winner Sorvino
92 Future moss
94 Tax form, to a Roman?
95 Sea off N Australia
96 *Home of Boris and Natasha*
99 Word on a candy heart
102 Hubbub
103 Salad fish
104 Baggage checker's org.
105 "___ We Got Fun"
106 Author Silverstein
107 Room at sea
110 Way to blow or flow: abbr.
112 *Bullwinkle's "master of misinformation" segment*
115 ___ disadvantage
116 Sworn obligation
118 Mythical goat-man
119 Lennon's love
120 *The school in the football episode, ___ U.*
123 *Voice of Bullwinkle (and Dudley Do-Right, and others)*
128 *The time-traveling canine*
129 Should that be the case
130 Lab gel
131 Claims
132 Other than me
133 Beatty and Buntline
134 Having "it"

DOWN

1 Modifying wd.
2 Pollster Harris
3 Cheesecake
4 She left "SNL" in 2000
5 Motel-sign letters
6 Lendable part?
7 Early calculator
8 Silky synthetic
9 Slays, slangily
10 Name in Notre Dame lore
11 Breaks down
12 Philly a.m. dish
13 Protruding
14 CPA's suggestion
15 Peach ___
16 Meriting a 10
20 Cobb and Detmer
22 With micro, library material
24 Snorter's quarters
27 State founder
30 "___ the morning!"
31 Comics-page Viking
32 Sister of Clio
33 Televise
34 Dough leavener
35 Actor Tom
37 It's human, they say
41 List ender
43 Part of HRH
46 Red opening?
47 1983 Tom Cruise-Shelley Long film, "___ It"
48 Cozy places
49 Be petty
50 Hostile party
52 Top left PC key
53 "Shut up!"
55 Road rig
59 Cell at sea
60 Doing zip
61 Lumberjacks
62 Take away
66 ___ muffin
67 Actress Cheryl
69 It may be re-inkable
70 Sound portion
71 Apply (pressure)
73 State's second-in-command: abbr.
74 Coffee additive, in Italian
75 Quartz variety
81 New Haven collegian
83 Page of music
85 Spitting bullets
86 Cozy places
87 Maximum poker bet
88 City on the Missouri
89 Serenade Heidi, maybe
90 Oddly amusing
92 Roget wd.
93 "___ spontaneous tomorrow" (Steven Wright)
97 Fountain treats
98 "___ Rock"
100 Game with 108 cards
101 German rockets of WWII
105 Cuts like ___
106 Larry was one
107 Crow's cry
108 Molecule parts
109 Iraqi port
111 Sleeping-pill brand
113 1990s Treasury chief Robert
114 Early Peruvians
117 Actor Ethan's ex
118 Bonnie portrayer
121 Wire wearer
122 Passing desires?
124 Trip need?
125 Part of UCLA
126 Put a strain on
127 Put a strain on

NOTE: *Two of the twelve hidden theme words in this puzzle are normally written with hyphens and are a bit lesser known. However, "sighting" the other ten should be easy.*

ACROSS

1 Crave
5 Doorway sides
10 Bit of AAA info
13 Ex-Tunisian rulers
17 Ex-Iranian ruler
18 Current location?
19 Unfriendly
21 Dr. Alzheimer
23 Greets, in a way (5)
25 Drink made with vodka, ginger beer, and lime (4)
27 Cracks an "ironclad" contract, perhaps (5)
29 A ___ bit
30 Buzzing
33 The Cards, on scoreboards
34 "Put ___ on it!"
35 Serious errors
36 Pushes past the guards, e.g.
38 Skim the clouds
40 1945 summit site
41 Like C. Dickens
42 Green field
44 Green-light alternatives (4)
48 Purveyors of rockabilly, British-style (5)
53 Monumental meal
54 Writer Anita
55 *Printemps* follower
56 Kids' guessing game
57 City on a fjord
61 Style maven José
62 Warm comfort, in Psalms 119 (4)
66 Firing tool?
67 Tenn. hours?
69 Brings in
70 Rooibos, for one
71 Tommy follower
72 "No man can ___" (9)
76 It became free of France in 1949
78 Show starter
79 Is scathing toward
80 Ida. neighbor
81 Work with flour
82 Leaning
84 Grumpy (6)
89 Punishment imposer, perhaps (5)
93 An ___ triple
94 Tornado heading, perh.
95 John who toured with Joel
96 Brit's eternity
98 Mineral that geologists hunger for?
101 Imperfectly made item
102 Soft-watch painter
105 Bygone bird
107 12-step spinoff group
108 Open-mouthed look
109 Type of picture (12)
113 Harrison's nickname (5)
115 Theme of this puzzle (and a theme answer as well) (4)
119 Columnist Goodman
120 Kans. neighbor
121 O'Connor's successor
122 At any time
123 Hand-held harp
124 Country group Diamond ___
125 Drive off
126 Damp at dawn

DOWN

1 See 94 Across
2 "It was you!"
3 Of CPOs and such
4 Chew ___
5 Hayley's Oscar-winning dad
6 Got an A+ on
7 Sitcom diner
8 Tree decor
9 Slangy smellers
10 Do-Right's org.
11 "Don't be ___ on him"
12 The sun, to Sonorans
13 Jack and Margery
14 "Slippery" tree
15 Berle: "I wish I'd said that!" Gleason: "Don't worry, ___"
16 What "people" has
20 XXI times XXXI
22 Playground staple
24 Old letter opener
26 Exhaustive ref.
28 Prayer start
30 Slangy fivers
31 Done for
32 Lyricist half of a famous duo
35 The ___ the earth
37 Born
39 Loser to DDE
40 "Most certainly"
43 Genesis son
45 "The Bells ___ Mary's"
46 Transplants, in a way
47 Self-applauding cry
49 Adversary
50 The police, e.g.
51 Sergeant-___
52 Mythical lion's home
56 Newspaper extra
58 Natural mood alterer
59 August signs
60 Giant stand-out
61 Office VIP
62 When you're ready
63 Ballet step
64 Author Sinclair
65 Bush or Kerry, e.g.
66 Simile middle
68 Busy retail area
73 Broadcasting giant
74 Steve Martin's nose-pinching invention in "The Jerk," the ___-Grab
75 Aft area
77 92 Down's loc.
81 Aspen rescue unit
83 Foil material
84 Em or jay follower
85 Bakery lure
86 Wizards' org.
87 Golden Rule preposition
88 Spotted
89 Campaign event
90 Rancor
91 How prices may rise
92 Safari getaway
97 Unrelated to battle
99 He's Ben, in *Star Wars*
100 Exhausted, to a southerner?
102 The present mo.?
103 Admirer's signoff
104 Unsociable sort
106 Robin Hood chum Allan-___
109 "Stand by Me" singer ___ King
110 Architect Saarinen
111 "Take ___ from me"
112 Celebrate
114 According to
116 Hadrian's "hi"
117 Lucky number?
118 Attempt

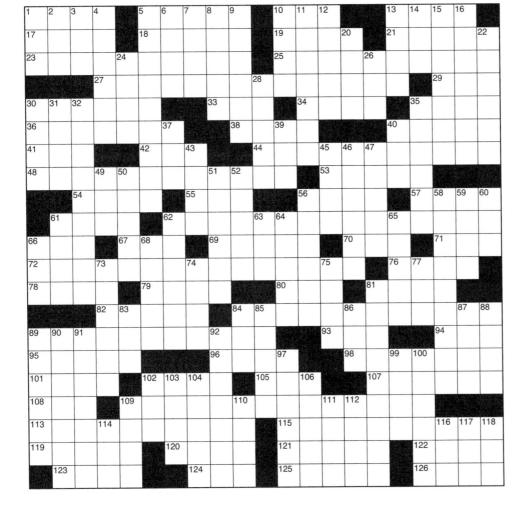

39 The Wright Frame of Mind

...Weird and logical at the same time

NOTE: *This puzzle contains a typically offbeat quip from comic Steven Wright (one you may have even heard), but since it took up so little space in the grid I decided to "open up" the grid and make the puzzle a bit of a challenger. So if you find yourself smiling and cursing at the same time, that's why.*

ACROSS

1 Depresses, slangily
8 Gestures
15 Attacks with snowballs
20 "What ___?!"
21 "... ___, k-i-s-s-i-n-g"
22 Works that seem to move
23 Thing that restrains
24 Tickle pink
25 Devotee
26 Old British guns
27 Places for French lessons
29 Enjoy free-falling
31 Trace
32 Stiller's partner
33 Early calculator of pi
36 Prov. on Niagara Falls
37 Loggins and ___
39 Beatles tune, "Fixing ___"
40 Fool
41 *Start of a Steven Wright quip*
43 Things that give off fragrances, for example
46 Fragrances
48 Give off
49 Puzzlemaking term for a two-letter unit
53 *Quip, Part 2*
58 Luzianne rival
59 "And ___ goes"
60 Vertigo setting
61 Grass you unroll
62 Like Heidi
63 *Quip, Part 3*
66 Washer phase
68 Draught pick
69 "Alley ___"
70 Move quickly
71 Part of the iris
72 *Quip, Part 4*
78 Hole for a shoelace
79 Crucifix inscription
80 Factory store
81 Most Scroogelike
84 *End of the quip*
88 Blood-group letters
91 Asian nursemaids
92 Weasel cousins
94 Babe's mom, e.g.
95 Thorny plant with small fruit clusters
98 Dusting or dishwashing
99 Signature follower, often
100 Sting in a tingling way
101 Corkscrew pasta
103 French opera composer Daniel
104 Actor Ryan
105 An essential vitamin, variantly
108 Number on a letter
110 Ninny's lack
111 Citrus hybrid
112 Bess's predecessor
113 Politico Kefauver
114 Dead Sea ascetics
115 Gordon of jazz and Manley of football

DOWN

1 Big name in ballet
2 Joining
3 Keepsake
4 Francis or Patrick
5 Remnants for Rover
6 Arapaho foe
7 The Stooges, e.g.
8 Skater Ito
9 Narrowed due to roadwork, perhaps
10 Yarn that's spun?
11 "___ far far better thing ..."
12 Club or soc.
13 O.T. book
14 Basket made with both hands
15 Like nylon, chemically
16 Lyric poem
17 "Livin' ___ Loca"
18 The doctor in "The Elephant Man"
19 Workplace woe
28 Algiers area
30 Unit of pressure
32 Improvement, to Jose (anagram of MARJOE)
34 Arrested
35 Article of property, sometimes used pejoratively
37 Callender and others
38 "What can I do ya for," e.g.
42 White House occupants of 1910
44 Showing love
45 Abbr. for Bilko
47 Pt. of CBS
50 Fatty Arbuckle, really
51 Variety of alpine pine
52 "Frankly, ___ ..."
53 Certifiable
54 "What Kind of Fool Am I" singer
55 Has a mind like ___ (forgets easily)
56 Risk-taker's second thought
57 Fleeting fashion
63 Lethal wrapper
64 Piano type
65 Infamous spy plane
66 Willies
67 Streisand film
69 Ideal
71 Actress Dahl
73 High-level transit
74 Tries to solve again
75 Jewish turnover
76 "Annie Get Your Gun" star, 1950
77 "Like a patient ___ upon a table" (T.S. Eliot)
82 "Tea for Two" singer
83 Touch-oriented
85 Dry ___
86 French wine region
87 Servants with water jugs
88 Place side by side
89 Edd who played Kookie on "77 Sunset Strip"
90 Familiarize
93 Horned chargers
96 On ___ (investigating)
97 In ___ (furious)
99 Old gold coin
102 Sign to interpret
103 Highest point
106 Suffers from
107 Bus. with many policies
109 Text addition

...Jerry: "I think you may have something here"

ACROSS

1 Arnold of "True Lies"
4 "Coffee Cantata" composer
8 ZIP ___
12 Russian fighter
15 She sang on "Double Fantasy"
16 Former Mogul capital
17 With Lodge, a famous chain
19 ZERO ___
21 Memorable "Seinfeld" quote
25 Dark brew
27 Boxer's aim
28 Em or Jay follower
29 ZIP ___
31 Part of a fault line?
32 Snake River state
35 Trig function
36 ___ consequence
37 NOTHING ___
41 Works on a soundtrack
43 Military training acad.
44 Move, to a Realtor
45 Vaqueros' ropes
47 Folk tales and such
49 ___ NOTHING
53 ___ ZERO
54 Scoffer's cry
55 Root beer brand
56 Early synthesizers
58 NOTHING ___

63 Humiliate
64 Sleeper's woe, to a Brit
66 "It's either them ___"
67 Highest U.S. military award: abbr.
69 Big tippler
70 Adler of Sherlock Holmes stories
71 Dog to beware of
73 Ingredient in a Greek 61 Down
74 Fall (behind)
75 Hike: abbr.
76 Answers with attitude
78 ___ NOTHING
79 ___ ZERO
82 Penicillin sources
83 Highway headache
84 Wildcatter's find
85 Old-womanish
87 ___ NOTHING
88 ZERO ___
90 Brand of microwavable dinners
92 German author and film star von Harbou
94 ZIP ___
95 Greek earth goddess
97 NOTHING ___
102 Lincoln and others
104 Attention-getter

106 Final preceders
107 A pal of Pooh
108 NOTHING ___
111 Small invader
112 Thai bills
114 With Proctor, an appliance maker
115 ZERO ___
119 Equine patriarch
120 V-shaped cut
121 Major intro
122 Veep before Al
123 Orgs. with patrol cars
124 NOTHING ___
125 Boris Godunov, for one
126 Old preposition

DOWN

1 NOTHING ___
2 Punctual
3 ZERO ___
4 "I Got You" follower
5 In the past
6 Key
7 "I ___ do it" (Alvin York)
8 Corp. VIP
9 Columbus's mo.
10 Qatar's capital
11 Authors Bagnold and Blyton
12 Japanese soup

13 Top Ten Genesis hit, "___ Deep"
14 ___ NOTHING
18 Lake near Syracuse
20 Subtlety
22 Sighed line
23 "Sans ice, bartender"
24 Biological subdivision
26 Pres. Jefferson
30 Belle of the ball
33 ___ NOTHING
34 Threatening words
38 Wipe out
39 Crossed paths
40 ___ Tomé
42 Closes with a bang
46 Prefix with light or night
48 A measure of resistance
49 Shoulder warmer
50 Of a leg bone
51 Fall color
52 Bit of Baja bread
53 Beethoven's German birthplace
54 ZERO ___
56 Walk in step
57 "La Bohème," e.g.
59 Famous
60 Salad green, garden ___
61 Egg dish
62 In
65 ___ ZERO
68 Silent screen star?
70 Worldwide, briefly
72 Capri, for one
73 Movies, slangily
75 "___ the Body Electric"
77 Great grade
78 Shed ___
80 Mrs. Porker
81 "Platoon" setting
86 Lincoln's home: abbr.
87 Human cannonball catcher
88 Leigh in "A Streetcar Named Desire"
89 ZIP ___
90 Composer Franz
91 "___ Down the Road"
92 Sliced into narrow strips
93 Prynne et al.
94 Hoods' rods
96 Darwinian ancestor
98 Govt. agent
99 Russia's ___ Mountains
100 NOTHING ___
101 Chop shop arrival
103 Bergen's dumbest dummy
105 Hawk's claw
109 Former partners
110 Noggin, in Nice
112 80 Down's mate
113 Word in a New Year's Day song
116 Some colas
117 Satisfied sounds
118 Free TV spot, e.g.

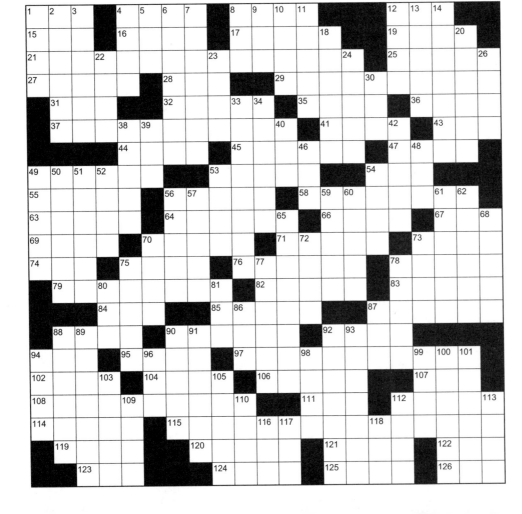

41 Something in Common
...One of the first puzzles I made for 23 Across

ACROSS

1 Felt
7 Farm butter?
10 Wrigley's field
13 Sofa scratcher
16 Fumbling folks
18 Tot's cry
19 Slangy negative
21 Personal account?
22 "Easter Parade" star
23 _ _ _ _
26 _ _ _ _
28 City in SW Russia
31 Had something
32 Be in the red
33 Church areas
34 _ _ _ _
39 Bemoan
42 Certain terminal
43 Scoreless score
45 U.K. record label
46 Cheese lover
49 Jazz joint job
50 _ _ _ _
57 Start of a Steinbeck title
59 Got there first
60 Curtain fabric
61 Portent
62 Circles overhead?
65 Cummerbund
66 Earnest appeals
67 _ _ _ _
71 _ _ _ _ _
74 Music partner?
75 Noisy god
77 Jughead's pal
78 Peek follower
79 Instrument that measures thickness
82 Aggravated one's condition?
83 Hill's partner?
87 _ _ _ _ _
91 Tampa, for one
92 Part of a coop group
93 Raw material
94 Early "Tonight Show" host
95 Extent
97 Underdog victories
100 _ _ _ _
104 Liqueur flavoring
107 Chef's bottleful
109 SpongeBob's home
110 Reef lurkers
111 _ _ _ _ _
118 _ _ _ _
119 Written LIKE THIS
123 Pre-citizenship course: abbr.
124 Hops-drying oven
125 Author Ferber
126 Frenetically
127 "The Thin Man" co-star
128 Big Red, once
129 They're right in front of U
130 Tests one's metal?

DOWN

1 Music from a Kingston trio?
2 Some rail transit
3 Filbert, for one
4 Like poker chips, often
5 Singer Pinza
6 Of the skin
7 First name in ragas
8 "You said it!"
9 Asia-crossing guy
10 ___ pig
11 Types of TV broadcast signals
12 "Heinz 57"-type dog
13 Letterman's letters?
14 Way to the altar
15 Bennett and Randall
17 Nasal partitions
18 Extinct bird
20 Resort village near the Kennedys' home
24 Chickens, ducks, etc.
25 Course for a Dr.-to-be
27 Kareem, before
28 Legally old enough
29 Reaction to the Beatles
30 City palls
35 German article
36 Start of the work wk.
37 Part of Welk's intro
38 *Rouge* alternatives, in roulette
40 Samoa studier Margaret
41 Tube prize
44 Korbut et al.
46 Shakespeare teen
47 ___ of faith
48 Drama-filled
51 Night predators
52 Sexy toon with a garter
53 Without moving
54 "I Won't ___ Day Without You"
55 Receive in a will
56 Handmade, as cigars
58 Putting on ___ (showing off)
63 Two of racing's Unsers
64 Company founded by Rockefeller
66 Greek letter
67 Up to one's ears (in)
68 Aristocratic
69 Vault line, in architecture
70 High infield fly
72 Light brown
73 Recalled diet aid, Fen-___
76 Label anew
79 Community-activity bldgs.
80 "Hard ___!" (helm command)
81 MGM sound effect
84 Ranking higher than
85 Campaign-button spot
86 Watchful ones
88 "Love is all I ever ___ find here" (John Denver)
89 To's opposite
90 Upper-left PC key
96 Forces
97 Computer customer
98 ___ the cleaners
99 Letter start
101 Abbr. on stamps
102 Sherpa's home
103 Showy perennial
104 Photographer Adams
105 Untrue
106 "The Boot"
108 Pariah
112 Study at the last minute
113 "For ___ jolly good ..."
114 Huge Brit. references
115 Lady's escort
116 Vitamin bottle abbr.
117 BPOE members
120 Docs' grp.
121 Settle (up)
122 Radical '60s grp.

...Pardon the interruptions

ACROSS

1 Vegan protein option
5 Urban rumblers
8 Jumped
13 Guys in sties?
18 Word with horse or soap
20 Failed line in tic-tac-toe
21 First name in 1950s news
22 Possible lagoon entrance
23 Illusion
26 Adrian portrayer
27 Not gross
28 CD-___
29 Well-established
30 Mix
32 Hillary's designation, once
33 Robert of "The 39 Steps"
35 Mathis classic
37 Land with a sultan
39 Fancy
45 Michael of "Arrested Development"
46 Waist material?
47 Posteriors
48 Like some pads or opinions
49 Needing no Rx
50 Brno-born
53 ___-appropriate
55 Hurry, old-style
56 Time to attack
58 Non-working condition?: abbr.
59 It merged with AT&T in 2005
61 Get cozy
64 Stealthily, in a way
66 Fridge sound
68 "Move it"
70 Lower-class, to a Brit
71 Created by craftspeople, as furniture
74 The FBI's guys
78 Winter hat feature
80 Yiddish word of disgust
81 "Ditto"
83 Mr. Bumble's position in "Oliver Twist"
86 Electronic games inits.
88 Dell rival
90 Beethoven's Third
91 You might hear yodeling on one
92 Dresser wood
94 American and Southwest
97 German article
98 Deer sirs
101 Britney Spears tune, "(I've Just Begun) Having ___"
103 I love, to Lupe
104 Queen's subjects
105 Arena of sorts
110 Hitch or glitch
111 Pool or puddle sound
112 "Nothing ___ importance"
113 Suitable for everyone, on the tube
115 "Fire" stone
117 1773 "jetsam"
119 Soul, to Sartre
120 Deletes, with "out"
123 Camel-filling stations
125 Like this word, dictionary-wise
129 Place for a bracelet
130 Chalet renter, perhaps
131 Taken ___
132 Hacienda material
133 "Prime Time" Sanders
134 "Playboy of the Western World" penner
135 WSJ alternative
136 Supreme knowledge test

DOWN

1 Hamlet's realtive
2 Frequent visitor to a TV sheriff's office
3 Had a hunch
4 Modern address
5 Giuliani, e.g.
6 Building site
7 Arty area of the Big Apple
8 Annie Hall's pet expression
9 Physicist Teller: abbr.
10 Present ___ grievances
11 Pale-looking
12 Brave's home, variantly
13 Comedy routine
14 Out with one's sweetie
15 Lasting from 6 p.m. to 6 a.m.
16 Ranch restraint
17 Judge's order
19 Yank who seems to be perennially in the news
24 Chaplin's last wife
25 "Tickle Me" doll
31 Wade foe
33 ___ testing
34 Mountain-climbing aid?
36 Beats in an upset
38 Voice of Bugs and Daffy
39 Brief fisticuffs
40 Ragamuffin
41 ___ to (encourage)
42 Menu boast, NO ___
43 Get thye goods on
44 TV show set at McKinley High
45 Cagney's Oscar role
50 Shared
51 Metal in Montana's motto
52 "Okay, break ___!"
54 Navy rank: abbr.
57 Alternative view, briefly
60 Meaningless chatter
62 Ham-and-___ (oafs)
63 Mediocre
65 Immigrant's subj.
67 Weekdays only: abbr.
69 Asian holiday
72 Monkey business
73 Israel's Golda
75 A fair individual?
76 Was the host of
77 Approaches
79 Early automaker's initials
82 Tee follower
83 Thai currency
84 Where Goliath was slain
85 Lodge social
87 Place to sweat it out
89 Old-style copy mach.
93 Owner of red, white, and blue planes, on the NYSE
95 Like a manager's special, perhaps
96 Like some insurance
99 Citrus hybrid
100 The bus stops here: abbr.
102 Temp worker, e.g.
104 Purchase
106 It may be colossal
107 Kojak's first name
108 Way off a freeway
109 Eminently draftable
113 Warty amphibian
114 Windmill part
116 Sour ending
118 Similar (to)
120 Microsoft game system
121 Island of exile
122 Appear
124 Six-yr. term holder
126 Relay-race part
127 Adverb ending
128 Tangy drink suffix

Early Puzzles

No, the puzzles on the following pages don't date back quite that far, but with 2013 being the crossword's 100th birthday, I thought I'd pick out a few puzzles from my black-and-white past that were either personal firsts or just special in some way. The publication dates on these range from 1980 to 2008.

Each one has a backstory, which is described on the page opposite each puzzle. In order to not spoil the solving experience, some of the descriptions begin in this section but continue on the solutions page, so you can read them after you've solved the puzzles. In any event, I hope the background notes help explain what on earth I was thinking. —MR

Marquees After the Storm

This may have been the first-ever drop-a-letter theme in a standard American crossword. If so, my apologies.

I was living in San Francisco in March 1978 when I read a news story about a crossword tournament that had just been held in Stamford, Connecticut. I thought, wow, if they have a second one, I am going. And as if to make me pay for using "eon" so many times in crosswords, the next year passed like one.

Finally, *finally*, the following March arrived and I took the red-eye from San Francisco to the East Coast to attend the second tournament. I had entered as a contestant, but I was really going for three reasons — to meet the grand dame of crosswords, puzzle editor Margaret Farrar, who would be handing out the prizes (and to whom I'd sold my first New York Times puzzle 13 years earlier), to meet Will Shortz, the host of the event who had just become an editor at GAMES magazine, and to generally hobnob with puzzle constructors who I knew only from their bylines.

(In those early days my puzzles could be a little wild and I had just sent a puzzle to Margaret that contained the made-up expression OWES A HUG. She rejected the puzzle for that entry — and about 20 other entries — but when we met for the first time in the lobby of the Stamford Marriott her first words were, "Do I owe you a hug or do you owe me a hug?")

This turned out to be a massively memorable weekend. Highlights included meeting Margaret and Will and a new crop of friends (you know who you are — Doug, Helene, Nancy, Mike, Stephanie, Jon, David, Stan, Mel, and many, many others.) I even finished third in the tournament. However, not being a speed solver at heart, I thought I'd feel more comfortable as a constructor for the event rather than a competitor. I had a theme idea I'd been thinking about for quite a while, made the puzzle, sent it to Will, he liked it, and that became my first tournament puzzle. It appeared at the 1980 event and is reprinted at right.

About the puzzle: The idea of taking a title or name or common expression and intentionally altering it by one or more letters for humorous effect had long struck me as a great idea for a crossword theme. Today, this type of change-a-letter, drop-a-letter, add-a-letter theme is pretty common, even ones that involve multiple letters, whole words, and even sounds, but in 1980, despite having solved hundreds of puzzles myself in a wide variety of magazines and books, I'd never seen one. So "Marquees After the Storm" may have been the first puzzle of this type ever to appear. If anyone finds a puzzle of this type that appeared before March 1980, I'll amend this paragraph in the second edition.

43 Marquees After the Storm

ACROSS

1 Mysterious
7 Pain for a princess?
10 ___ stick
14 Medical term for St. Vitus's Dance
15 Smoother
17 "Empire of the Ants" co-feature?
19 Ms. Barrett
20 Silly
21 Eaglets' home
22 Commerce watchdog: abbr.
23 Run-through that releases radiation, briefly
25 Tiny, furry pet
27 "Green Slime" co-feature?
30 Confused comment
31 Gives guns to
33 Shriver of tennis
36 Purina rival
38 "Of Human Bondage" co-feature?
40 City near Pompeii
43 Rocky rival
44 Type of truck
45 "Close Encounters" co-feature?
47 Commandment word
48 Commit a foul
49 Junction, of sorts
50 City opposite Dover
54 "Francis the Talking Mule Goes to West Point" co-feature?
58 Sends again
63 Out of the way
64 ___-de-lance
65 Europe/Asia boundary
66 Circle parts
67 Former name of the KGB
68 "The Blob" co-feature?
73 Crossword words, sometimes
74 Anesthetics
75 M. Descartes
76 Stout relative?
77 Give ___ (ogle)

DOWN

1 Five ___ shadow
2 "The Razor's Edge" co-feature?
3 Actress Imogene
4 Suffix for "fail"
5 Luau garb
6 Bicycles built for two
7 Gasp
8 Climax
9 Pitcher drink
10 Homonym for a synonym of "buckets"
11 Works that play with your vision
12 Aladdin's lamp jockey
13 Judge's shout
15 The S sound in "cent"
16 Baby carriage
18 Attended
19 First word of three John Wayne movies
23 Ice org.
24 Overly
25 Ruffled, as feelings
26 Let in or let on
28 Whac-___ (arcade game)
29 What stripes indicate
32 Darn, for example
33 "Blood Alley" co-feature?
34 Words after "here" or "there" in a song
35 Food folder
36 Stake in the game
37 Actor Bert
38 Coffee dispenser
39 Design feature
41 Curve
42 "Crime" on the diamond
43 Doll's word
46 Famous Willie
50 The first to stab Caesar
51 Start of an Ella Fitzgerald standard
52 Israeli airport city
53 Wood splitter
55 Actions determining fate
56 Tranquility
57 Actress Joanne
58 Queen, e.g.
59 Uneven, as leaf edges
60 Georgia city
61 Winged
62 ___ of Man
66 Buffet type with unlimited seconds: abbr.
67 Architectural curve
69 Bikini top
70 OPEC's thing
71 Bible verb ending
72 The aforementioned miss

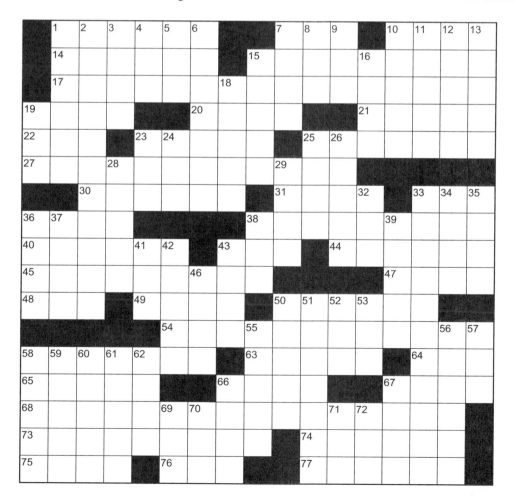

On the Golden Gate

I have this strange pattern of not getting a puzzle job in the city where I lived until after I moved to a different city. From 1962 to 1976 I lived in Tucson, Arizona, but my puzzle didn't start appearing in Tucson's paper, the Arizona Daily Star, until I moved to San Francisco. After leaving San Francisco for Los Angeles in 1979 I got the San Francisco Examiner job. After leaving Los Angeles for Tampa in 1993 I got the Los Angeles Times job. Just weird.

In any event, the story of how I got my very first weekly newspaper gig — for the San Francisco Examiner in October 1985 — is told in detail in the foreword to one of my earlier books ("Sunday Crosswords, Volume 5"). In brief, I got the job because the first person who was contacted, who lived in Connecticut, had used the word TERRIER in her audition puzzle, and the Examiner took note that the simplest of letter changes would have turned it into PERRIER, "a more appropriate West Coast answer." Could they recommend a person with a more California turn of mind? When my phone rang in Santa Monica I couldn't pick it up fast enough.

My first puzzle for the Examiner was (don't be shocked) full of puns on the subject of (let me think) the Golden Gate Bridge. It appeared on October 6, 1985, in the premiere issue of the Examiner's new magazine, called Image. Eddie De Bartolo Jr., who owned the Forty Niners at the time, was on the cover. He now lives about 15 miles from me in Tampa. The puzzle is about six inches away from here, on the right.

44 On the Golden Gate

ACROSS

1 Hold everything?
6 Starting
10 British gun
14 Nth degree
17 "How much then is a man better than ___?" (Matt. 12:12)
19 Olympian Johnson
21 "Sidewalk inspector"
22 Ring great
23 Golden Gate query?
26 Sun. sermon giver
27 Golden Gate reference book?
29 "This ___ sudden!"
30 Swearing-in word
31 "Golden" principle
33 Pundit
36 Poisons
37 Adjudged
41 Beach acquisition, perhaps
42 Footnote abbr.
45 32-card game
46 Sewing case
47 Prayer need, for some
48 We, *non?*
49 Golden Gate support?
53 Avoids wasting
55 Central figure in the My Lai incident
57 Greek cross
58 Caviar
59 A pretty girl isn't like one
61 New York city
62 Bantu native of Kenya
64 Engineering feat of the Golden Gate?
70 Winter hazard
71 Grave robber
72 Health writer Davis
73 Bomb throwers?: abbr.
76 Believer's suffix
77 Dominated the scene
79 Salmon's tail?
80 Operates like the Golden Gate?
83 Himalayan goat
85 Scandinavian airline
86 See 42 Across
87 Other rtes.
88 Barry, Robert, or Samuel
89 Its definition is often debated
90 Ford, to Nixon, on 9/8/74
92 Godless one
95 Area meas.
97 John ___, the Lone Ranger
98 Otological fellows
100 It's 2,100 mi. WSW of San Francisco
102 Sidewalk to the Golden Gate?
108 Sign-off to singleness
110 Golden Gate-at-rush hour comment?
112 In favor of
113 Approximately
114 Lawn invaders
115 Nobel poet Pablo
116 Languished
117 Authority figure
118 Gab or slug follower
119 Controversial H.S. subj.

DOWN

1 Hem's companion
2 Safety watchdog: abbr.
3 Literary monomaniac
4 Cut anew
5 Ruling
6 "Rule, Britannia!" composer
7 Small desert denizen
8 Carl Sagan's "The Dragons ___"
9 An Alou
10 Japanese mushroom
11 Pop group or famous dog
12 Black, to Byron
13 What Clint had in spaghetti westerns
14 "The Maltese Falcon" co-star
15 Dorchester drink
16 Louis who said, *"L'état, c'est moi"*
18 They're jocularly called "phony doctors"
20 Makes into tiny pellets
24 In the past
25 BART stop: abbr.
28 Darn it again?
32 Surgeon intro
33 Uses ukuleles
34 One-time Wisconsin-based insurance giant
35 California players
36 Dog yummy
38 ___ reindeer
39 Hothouses for humans
40 Dam thing
43 South Pacific resident
44 Meat amount
45 Sneaky
49 Have one's arms around, sometimes desperately
50 The measure of proof?
51 "Don't ___!" ("Wise up!")
52 Shot the rapids, perhaps
54 Numskulls
56 From ___ Z
60 Pastrami parlors
62 Unit of TNT force
63 Sailing term
65 Pay up
66 Flop
67 "You ain't kiddin'!"
68 Wide receiver Henry who played with the L.A. Rams, 1983-93
69 Eating events
73 Swab brand
74 De Brunhoff's elephant
75 Squaw Valley info
77 San Francisco's are famous: abbr.
78 Nasser's old org.
81 Paul as a pool player
82 Overlapping parts, in music
84 Pushes again
88 Runs
91 "Goldfinger" hat-hurler
92 Pater of Paris
93 "I'm ___ my word"
94 Lamblike
96 Old word meaning "question"
99 Curve
100 Choose
101 "East of Eden" brother
103 Continent combiner
104 Air-leak sound
105 Dennis, to Mr. Wilson
106 Essential idea
107 Conceal
108 Conditions
109 Edmond O'Brien film noir partly set in San Francisco
111 Teeny bit

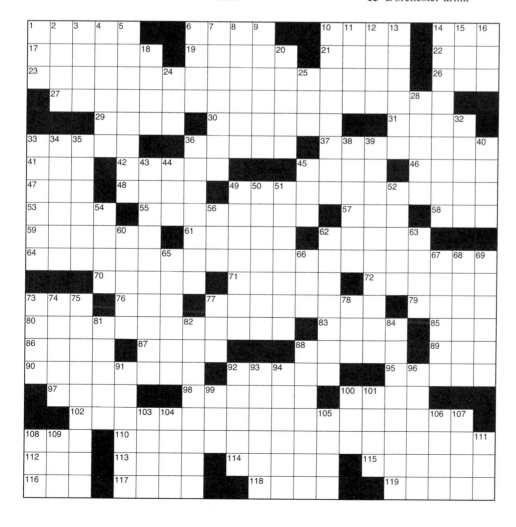

Tearfully Yours

After I'd been making the San Francisco Examiner puzzle for about five years I started to wonder if anyone in the Bay Area was really solving it or if my particular brand of humor and hijinks was outside most solvers' appreciation zone. At that time I hadn't quite learned yet that solvers usually don't write unless they're pointing out some bonehead mistake, such as mixing up Flatbush and Flushing, New York. (Not that I ever did that, of course.)

In 1990 I noticed that a certain special day was going to fall on a Sunday, so I decided to make the puzzle that appears at right. After it came out, so many letters came in that the entire letters page of the magazine was devoted to just the mail from this crossword. (One guy's letter began: "If I'd had a heart attack, you would've heard from my lawyer!" ... although I'm pretty sure his tongue was firmly planted in his cheek.)

(Important side note: Will Shortz was still the editor of GAMES magazine when this puzzle first appeared.)

Anyway, I hadn't planned it, but this was the puzzle that made Marie and me realize that Bay Area solvers were not only out there but that they were a very interesting, funny bunch, and very much on my wavelength. This was the puzzle that made us realize that syndication might be a genuine, viable possibility.

All we had to do was convince newspapers across the country to switch to a new Sunday crossword, and everybody knows how well that always goes over with readers.

45 Tearfully Yours

ACROSS

1 Quetzalcoatl Indian
6 Very, in music
11 Pull an all-nighter
15 Beaks
19 "Blue ___ Shoes"
20 Sacro ending
21 "Take this"
22 Tell ___ (fib)
23 *Why this is my last San Francisco crossword*
27 Buffoon
28 Actress-novelist Chase
29 Community property word
30 Large land
31 Mil. training site
32 Say "No thanks," e.g.
34 Bounder
36 Sault ___ Marie
37 See 23 Across
44 Author Bret
45 You're relaxed when you're at it
46 Without assistance
47 Singer Murray
48 Vicks ___ Rub
49 ___ dish
52 Big book
56 See 23 Across
61 Relief pitcher's stats
62 Crossword birds
63 Escape ___
64 Run into
67 Word to an unknown fellow
68 Feel the same way
69 TGIF eve
70 Small amount
71 Herb Alpert hit, "___ of Honey"
73 McGarrett's hi
74 Expressed displeasure
76 See 23 Across
82 Mideast VIP
83 Sailing dangers
84 Goddess of discord
85 With -rotatory, counterclockwise
86 Run ___ of the law
89 Ont. or Alta.
90 Take the wheel
91 See 23 Across
98 Extinct bird
99 Go bad
100 Carry-on ___
101 ALF's cousins
102 Actress Jessica
104 PDQ cousin
105 Unseat
107 However, briefly
110 See 23 Across
116 Gung-ho
117 Throneside instrument
118 Wet spot?
119 Two under par
120 Misspeaks, e.g.
121 A woodwind
122 Blood info
123 Small measures

DOWN

1 Warts and all
2 S California beach
3 Heat level, briefly
4 Conductor de Waart
5 Cold-fish appetizer
6 Weasel's relative
7 Ms. Korbut
8 Did the fuse
9 Chinese ideal
10 Ink shooters of the deep
11 She's quite a Ladd
12 Boys in gray
13 "Exodus" hero
14 Actress Ryan
15 Rabbit punch locale
16 Marty Robbins classic
17 Payment instruction
18 Appeared
24 Last customer Rick expected to see
25 Part of a ship
26 Eve or Elizabeth
31 Some music ensembles
32 Do some grass?
33 Farm female
34 Clive of "Frankenstein"
35 Latin I word
37 Yum woon sen cuisine
38 Dangle
39 Mr. Rubik
40 Less distant
41 Looks amazed
42 Challenges
43 "Understand?"
48 Scarlett portrayer
49 He won, but at great cost
50 Of a famous volcano
51 Bible pronoun
53 Drop out
54 Desert mountain
55 Founded: abbr.
57 "___ la vista"
58 Politely decline
59 Dumb rowdies
60 More faithful
64 Actress Martha
65 One little bit
66 Surfing mecca
68 Sailing term
69 Work nine ___
72 "Out!"
73 White poplar
74 "She Walks in Beauty" poet
75 Greek letters
77 Target for Teddy Roosevelt
78 Sleuth Wolfe and others
79 Swerve
80 Daredevil's first name
81 Actor Calhoun
87 Axed
88 Animal in a Mexican circus
89 Poe character
90 Came to an understanding
91 Teen's intro to almost any comment
92 Body shop offering
93 Bengal fighter
94 Countenance
95 Latin abbr.
96 Map out again
97 Ricky portrayer
103 Wins at cards
104 Periodic chart abbr.
105 Motherless child of TV
106 Sky bear
107 Forum wear
108 Actress Celeste
109 Corrida shouts
111 It may be inflated
112 San Francisco's ___ Hill
113 Bleachers shout
114 Coiler by a queen
115 "The ___ Side"

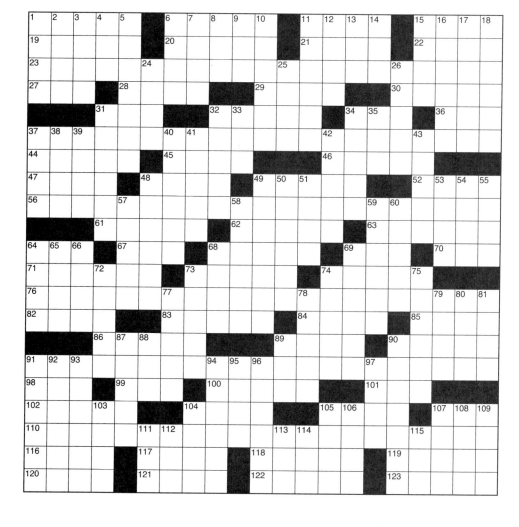

Terms of Engagement

This may have been the first-ever marriage-proposal crossword in a major newspaper.

In late 1991 I got a letter from a Stanford University grad named Neil M. Nathanson with an unusual request. He and his girlfriend, Leslie Hamilton, were fans of my Sunday crossword in the San Francisco Examiner — puzzle solving was one of the things that had brought them together — and now Neil wanted to pop the question. He said he'd been training Leslie to solve photostats of my Examiner puzzle in preparation for what he was about to ask: He wanted to know if I could make a marriage-proposal crossword that looked exactly like the Examiner's Sunday puzzle, layout, fonts and all, so that he could make a copy of it and present it to Leslie as if it were the real Sunday crossword. The difference would be that the main theme answers would turn out be his genuine proposal of marriage.

My immediate response was, somehow it had to be the real Sunday puzzle, not a photostat, and done in a way that Leslie would get the message loud and clear, but not the solving public. That is, regular solvers throughout the Bay Area would have to think that it's just another Sunday puzzle. I called Neil the next day and said I wasn't really sure how I was going to do this, but I had the germ of an idea.

I used to be a copy editor, so I'd been around newspaper offices long enough to know that when a paper has a Sunday magazine, it's almost always preprinted, and someone usually comes into the newsroom three or four days before Sunday and drops a stack of them on a table. It was the same with the Examiner Sunday magazine. So the plan was to make a puzzle with a generic "wedding checklist" theme — what to do if you're planning the Big Event — which anyone solving the puzzle could appreciate, but to also include, among the non-theme answers, eight or nine words related specifically to Leslie. They would be clued straight, but she was almost sure to catch on with so many personal references "accidentally" occurring in one puzzle.

But just to be absolutely certain we took one of the preprinted magazines, which, luckily, did arrive in the Examiner's office three days early, and, using expensive highlighter pens, we lightly colored in the squares that related to her and Neil — pink for her answers, light blue for the actual proposal. We then gave Neil that copy, he swapped it with the one in his regular Sunday Examiner, and then he picked up Leslie early that Sunday and drove her to a secluded spot in Yosemite. And it had to be early so that Leslie wouldn't have time to buy the paper herself.

Neil said he was sweating bullets the entire morning. As she calmly solved, Neil had to pretend to be interested in other parts of the paper, until she said, "Hey, this puzzle is all about me." Neil said, "Um, really?" Long story short, it worked like a charm, she said yes, and Neil later told us, "You know, we never did finish the crossword." Hmm ...

The next day the Examiner ran the story on Page 1, which prompted the Chronicle's Herb Caen to lead with it in his popular column on Wednesday. The Associated Press then picked it up from Caen and within a few days it was everywhere, including CNN, the "Today" show and People magazine.

And it was People that had the best closing line. When Neil said he didn't have a backup plan if the puzzle hadn't worked, the People reporter suggested he do it the normal way — "DOWN on one knee ... with a hand ACROSS his heart."

46 Terms of Engagement

ACROSS

1 "How ___ you?"
4 Sit-down string *
9 Be
14 PICK OUT ___
18 RENT ___
19 Stay away from
20 RESERVE ___
22 Scoreless score
23 STOCK UP ON ___
25 View with awe
26 Actress Garr
27 "Who's driving this car, you ___?"
28 Spicy holiday drink
29 Basher with bangs
30 CHOOSE ___
32 Eisenhower foe, initially
34 ___ tree (trapped)
36 Bill's partner?
39 The bride, e.g.
40 HIRE ___
42 Adorable dog *
45 All over again
48 State or quarterback *
50 Took a 3 Down
51 His home's on the range
53 San Francisco valley
55 Turkish official
56 They broke the ___ when they made you
58 French article
60 Face on a ten *
62 RENT ___
64 Sweetums *
66 Gene form
68 Crossword cookie
69 Looks from wolves
71 Actress Caron *
73 Pencil ends
75 With 78 Across, a modest proposal
78 See 75 Across
80 "Mother ___" (Irish song)
83 Loose ad in the newspaper
85 Singer Lopez
89 Arthur of tennis
90 Durocher's nickname, Leo ___
92 Astronaut Armstrong *
95 Glasgow guy
96 Palo Alto campus *
98 Photog's original
100 Hit by Cupid's arrow, old-style
102 Wedding words
103 Craggy peak
104 Lay ___ (bomb big-time)
106 Planter's product
108 City architect, in a way *
110 Big diamond, e.g.
112 CALL ___
115 Firewood
116 Rose *
118 Bar habitué
119 Spanish article
120 Yug. neighbor
121 CALL ___
125 Golf prop
127 Mil. rank
129 Cries of disgust
133 Environment
134 PLAN ___
137 BOOK ___
139 Flower girls, e.g.
140 "Tristram Shandy" author
141 Big-event hall
142 "___ can that be?"
143 Facility
144 Coin side
145 Scatter, as petals
146 This instant

DOWN

1 Sonny and Cher's early label
2 German industrial valley
3 Big test
4 Nurse topper
5 She rode Buttermilk
6 CBS' eye, for one
7 Tongue, in Latin
8 Love poem
9 The heights phobia
10 Chong's ex-partner
11 Last Hebrew letter
12 Mimic
13 Croat clasher
14 Awful
15 Liz Smith paragraph
16 Author Ephron
17 Enter
21 Bruce and Christopher
24 Intended
29 The Taj ___
31 Puppeteer Lewis
33 Waxed cheese
35 Home computers, briefly
37 Ending for "outrage"
38 ___ warpath
40 Lauren's guy
41 "What's in ___?" (Shak.)
42 See 5 Down
43 Lift?
44 Card controller
46 ___ nous (confidentially)
47 Suitor
48 Teen hangout, nowadays
49 Genesis land
52 Nail-file surface
54 Grandson of Adam
57 Actress Tyne
59 Snail trail
61 Successful dieters, maybe
63 "Where ___" (Rodgers & Hart classic)
65 Lubricate again
67 "When will I ever ___?"
70 "To ___, With Love"
72 Irving Berlin's "I Got the ___ the Morning"
74 Total: abbr.
76 Spill the beans
77 MacNeil's news partner
79 Highways and byways: abbr.
80 Sail support
81 Mary or John Jacob
82 "Coochie-coochie" guitarist-singer
84 Exhausted
86 121 Down topping
87 Knobby points
88 "Take ___ leave it"
91 Rims
93 Tiny terrors
94 Abner describer
97 Malingerer
99 Craftiness
101 7 feet, for example
105 Day-___ colors
107 Another dam project
109 "I ain't ___!" (Rocky Balboa)
111 Trouser line
113 Go to the wedding
114 Take to the wedding
117 Cotillion girls
120 Coeur d'___, Idaho
121 BUY ___
122 Song for one
123 Kennedy and Koppel
124 Sex adviser Dr. ___
126 1 Across, in French
128 Unique person: slang
130 PICK OUT ___
131 Twinkie alternative
132 Winter white
135 Charge
136 Monk's title
137 Possesses
138 Go off course, as a missile

Happy Birthday to Me

In 2003 my birthday happened to fall on a Sunday, which didn't seem like a big deal at the time, since I generally don't make crosswords about myself. But something else happened a month before that date. Marie and I were eating at an Outback steakhouse and one of the featured wines on the menu was, well, see 119 Across. It took me about a second to notice how doubly appropriate this particular wine was. Also, Sunday crosswords are traditionally 21 squares on a side and the name of this wine was exactly 21 letters long. So here I had a birthday coming up in a month that happened to fall on a Sunday and a puzzle answer that would be perfect. Maybe the puzzle gods were trying to tell me something.

Yes, they were telling me, "Go jump in a lake!" Or words to that effect, because for the next two weeks I got no sympathy from the puzzle gods whatsoever. To be precise, the symmetry thing wasn't working. (For you newbies, almost all crosswords are symmetrical along their diameters, which means that if you turn a crossword grid upside-down, the arrangement of black squares stays the same. This also means that every theme answer, except the one in the center, has to have a twin of the same length on the opposite side of the puzzle.) What I had was an eight-letter answer with no symmetrical twin and a nine-letter answer with no symmetrical twin. Plus, since I wanted the name of the wine to run near the bottom of the grid as sort of the payoff answer, I needed a matching 21-letter answer at the top. But no. Nothing was working. It was a puzzle with three dead ends.

Until I woke up in the middle of the night — it just hit me. And in one fell swoop a single theme answer solved all three issues. You'll see what it is when you solve 21 and 23 Across. (After you're done, see the further explanation in the solution section.)

47 Happy Birthday to Me

ACROSS

1 The ultimate motivator
5 Criticism
9 The Jetsons' dog
14 Battery terminal: abbr.
17 Like a.m. potatoes
19 Watering hole
21 Enigmatic pop star, with 23 Across
23 See 21 Across
26 Coastal
27 Cold spells
28 Eat like a rat
29 Ceremony words
30 Least loose
33 Hear here
34 Troy Donahue's real name (or the character he played in "The Godfather, Part II")
38 "___ Is Born"
42 His daughter became a boxer
43 Chart
44 Oscar-winning Judi
46 TV abbr.
47 "Emergency!"
50 Best's replacement
52 Seeking, in ads
54 Wrestling hold
57 Car type
58 Land amounts
61 Penniless
62 The Japanese colonel in "The Bridge on the River Kwai"
64 Gaucho's rope
66 Mr. Carnegie
67 Copy
70 1964 Disney film, "The Misadventures of ___"
73 Address locs.
74 Fir tree resin
77 ___ City, 116 Down
78 Printer's need
81 Ensign's answer
83 Do well
85 Commerce pact of the 1990s: abbr.
89 Lasting three hot months
91 Hard/rock insert
92 Fortify anew
93 Center opener
94 Baton Rouge sch.
95 Let out ___ (bellow)
98 Nav. rank
100 Montreal's prov.
101 Censor
103 Lasik surgery need
106 Lake, to Luigi
109 Beatles hit
111 Marin Co. special-effects house
112 Official Cookie of the American Crossword (according to me)
113 Tolerated
115 Nod
119 Popular brand of wine that's doubly apt for this puzzle
124 Noted Eastern conqueror
125 Hardcover?
126 Hot bath of a sort
127 Course abbr.
128 Lopsided wins
129 Visitor to Rick's place
130 Gift for young builders

DOWN

1 Really loud: abbr.
2 Love god
3 A million plus?
4 Send again
5 Quit, in cards
6 "The lofty city, he ___ it low" (Isaiah 26:5)
7 Be an inquirer
8 Relatives
9 Periodic chart info: abbr.
10 California peak
11 Class trial
12 Knocks
13 Ice great
14 Feather, in zoology
15 March prize
16 Oyster et al.
18 Brabantio's daughter
20 Lenient toward
22 Ty Cobb was one
24 Spanish wine
25 Tool for nuts
31 Choice words, perhaps
32 Utilize
34 Lander target of December 1999
35 Mr. Wiesel
36 Skin
37 Narcotic
39 Amounts
40 Up to ___ (able)
41 Brand of nasal spray
45 "It ___ Be You"
47 Goes bad
48 Eightsome
49 Distorts
51 Pump content
53 Zodiac sign
55 Bully boys
56 Inc., over there
59 Gray or Moran
60 Inasmuch as
63 Dunk
65 "The foaming cleanser"
67 Mortify
68 "Hand it over, pal"
69 Varnish resin
71 Ms. Doone
72 Intertwine
75 U.S. symbol
76 See 95 Across
79 They signed up
80 Actress Charlotte
82 Turn on a pivot
84 Indian for whom a sea is named
86 Oft-heard queries, online
87 No lie
88 Part of 85 Across
90 Gingerbread house visitor
96 Oxygen compounds
97 Do something
99 Geo model
101 Sot's problem
102 Malleable
104 Awards
105 Without principles
106 Hay places
107 Regions
108 "Don't ___ wrong ..."
110 They get planed
113 Singer Guthrie
114 Boyfriend
116 The Sooner St.
117 Chimney feature
118 Hawaiian senator, 1959-77
120 Go wrong
121 Beta Kappa lead-in
122 Marine critter
123 Chinese concept

Connecting Flights

Starting in March 2004 I made a series of crosswords for the inflight magazine of a certain well-known airline. The puzzle at right was the first one. The instructions ("How To Play") pretty much lay out your mission, should you decide to accept it. If you're still up in the air after you're finished, everything is explained on the puzzle's solution page.

48 Connecting Flights

HOW TO PLAY *Hidden diagonally in this puzzle's grid are the names of four cities that form **a perfect rectangle**. Can you 1) find all four, and 2) tell me what airline I took to visit them?*

ACROSS

1 Middle East gulf
5 Tricks container
8 Silly Putty container
11 Safety org.
15 Where your fodder is?
16 Wire service letters
17 Agent on HBO's "Entourage"
18 "Hold it!"
19 "Law & Order" star
22 Flier's stunt
23 "Mourning Becomes Electra" playwright
24 "Simpsons" character who got hooked on crosswords in a 2008 episode
25 Rich cake
26 Jam ingredient?
27 Get-up-and-go
29 Sexy dance
31 She played Rosemary
32 Most ventilated
34 Word said repeatedly by Alex Trebek
36 Violinist's need
39 Cassowary's cousin
40 Suspect's story
41 Men, in Marseille
43 Voice a view
45 Singer Paul
48 ___ budget
49 Sports page datum
51 Blocker and Brown
53 Drop of gel
54 Vaccine VIP
56 Manicurist's aid
58 Self-confidence
60 Last name in pharmaceuticals
62 Building wing
64 Fighting fiercely
65 Pod-bearing plant grown for forage
67 Oblong pastries
69 Word in San Francisco's motto
70 Medicinal plant
72 "Boy, is it cold!"
73 "Ready Brew" coffee introduced by Starbucks in 2009
76 Saturn features
78 Funny Dame
80 Moving like The Blob
82 Wiped-out bird
83 SUV ancestor
85 Staple of southern cooking
86 Mail carrier in Harry Potter books
87 Forest female
88 Needle bearer
89 Far cry from Joe Cool
90 Letters on Cardinals' caps
91 Spring mo.
92 Whole lot

DOWN

1 The NAACP, for one
2 1950s hit by 45 Across
3 Co-star of 1940's "A Wild Hare"
4 "Oh, ___ get it"
5 Gable, opposite Leigh
6 Imitate
7 Lopez-Affleck comedy, "Jersey ___"
8 Gnaws away on
9 Bad-pun reaction
10 Pink lady ingredient
11 Cold capital
12 Wintertime precaution rarely seen in California
13 ___ & the Blowfish
14 Come into view
20 Plants (like edelweiss) that can grow in cold climates
21 Prepares to take notice?
25 She's Tara on Showtime's "United States of Tara"
28 Rhubarb, for one
30 Ore of lead
32 Intention
33 Chew the scenery
35 Org. that helps entrepreneurs
36 Greek letters
37 Daughter of 23 Across
38 "I'm not surprised"
40 Santa ___, Calif.
42 Inscribed pillars
44 Pastoral poem
46 ___ Sutra
47 Short form, in its short form
50 Adams of "Julie & Julia"
52 Little bird
55 Tom Hanks's role on "Bosom Buddies"
57 Take back, as testimony
59 LAPD's Columbo et al.
61 Not as much
63 "CSI" setting, often
65 Police line
66 Baltimore player
67 Be-all's partner
68 Laundry worker
71 Package contents info, for short
73 Sentry's watch
74 Hole-___
75 Nixon veep
77 Well-behaved
79 Verdi opera
81 Microwaves: slang
83 Brillo competitor
84 Alley of the comics

At the Stamp Celebration

During a phone conversation with Will Shortz sometime in December 1997 he told me that the Post Office was coming out with a crossword puzzle stamp, the first one ever. It would be part of a series of stamp sheets called "Celebrate the Century" — the puzzle stamp, marking the invention of the crossword in 1913, was part of the 1910s decade sheet of 15 different stamps. The downside was that you had to buy the whole sheet of 15 different stamps just to get the one crossword stamp. (I've always thought the Post Office missed a sure-fire best-seller doing it this way. Puzzle fans would have bought millions of them.)

The sheets were scheduled to come out on Tuesday, February 3, 1998, but the stamp itself was being officially announced two days earlier on the crossword page of the Sunday New York Times, along with a picture of the stamp. So Will asked me if I could make a Sunday crossword as a tie-in with the announcement.

Here's where my little pocket notebooks come into play. I carry one everywhere I go — if I don't write down ideas immediately I will totally forget them. And one of my 1983 notebooks contained an idea for a stamp puzzle — not the whole puzzle, just the last three theme answers. But that's all I needed to build a puzzle around. The result was the crossword at right, which is one of the best puzzles I've ever made for the Times. And it took only 15 years to happen.

So remember, kids. Write things down and never throw a good idea away. Somehow, someday, its time will come.

(Extra special thanks to Will for stepping up big-time to help me get permission to reprint it.)

49 At the Stamp Celebration

ACROSS

1 Rum-soaked cake
5 Tall, slender hound
11 Practical joke
15 Bleached
19 12th century poet
20 Neckwear accessory
21 Uzbek sea
22 Fashion house ___-Picone
23 "At 9 a.m., breakfast will be supplied by ___"
25 Prohibit
27 Mastic, for one
28 "At 11 a.m. ___ will speak"
30 Comics sound
31 Unusually smart
34 First name in TV talk
35 Like R. L. Stine stories
36 "At 1 p.m. ___ will sing ..."
39 Govt. property org.
40 River near Chantilly
41 O'Donnell and Perez
42 "... a tune from one of their ___"
48 Modern office staples
49 Jackson and Leigh
50 Handle a joystick
51 In post-career mode: abbr.
52 Dance invitation response
53 Axis Powers, once
54 Jamaican sect member
56 "At 3 p.m., the President will ___ ..."
61 First name among sopranos
62 The less-used end
63 Nonexistent
64 Key of Mendelssohn's Symphony No. 3
66 Kind of alcohol
67 "... on the subject of ___"
74 Initiated, legally
76 Europe/Asia dividers
77 Actress Suzanne
78 Ambient music pioneer
79 Mount Vernon, e.g.
81 Wristbone-related
82 Abbr. on a Mayberry envelope
85 "At 5 p.m. the Philatelic Society will discuss some ___"
87 Knot-tying place
88 Actress Ward
89 Hosts
90 "And at 7 p.m. there will be a showing of the '60s film ___ ..."
92 Snail trail
95 Slick, so to speak
98 Some pops: abbr.
99 Wage news
100 "... starring ___ ..."
103 Goes limp
104 Call to action
105 "... unless ___"
110 Grouper grabbers
111 Numerous
112 Dario Fo forte
113 Infamous Roman
114 Cobbler's need
115 Places for coats
116 Lively intelligence
117 Jersey Standard's other name

DOWN

1 Conk
2 Without form
3 Without foundation
4 Gallery event
5 British gun
6 It can be fresh or hot
7 Singer Peggy
8 Put ___ fight
9 Brick baker
10 Dr. Scholl products
11 I love: Fr.
12 Ball partner
13 City on the Ganges
14 Basic: abbr.
15 Human-powered taxi
16 Province of Spain
17 Tongue-lasher?
18 Access
24 Ticket
26 Slangy tag-team member
29 TV dog
30 Boarding place
31 Sorry individual
32 Barcelona buck, once
33 Colorful spiral seashell
37 Mary of Peter, Paul and Mary
38 My, to Mimi
39 Lead pumper
42 [see other side]
43 Collins juice
44 Quite a while
45 Bearish
46 Underground systems
47 Fire escape route
49 Jupiter
50 "___, the heavens were opened" (Matt. 3:16)
52 Glove fabric
53 Film changes
55 Sheriff Lobo portrayer
56 Wound with sound
57 He's a weasel
58 Flatten
59 Talus area
60 Loss-prevention click
65 Blackbird
68 1984 Peace Nobelist
69 "Dies ___"
70 Familiars, often
71 Writer Singer and inventor Singer
72 Apathy
73 Drives forward
75 Prepare to land
80 Subj. of '60s protests
81 He helped topple Batista
82 Slaps a new head on
83 Dentists' kids, probably
84 Have the guts
86 Prodigious
87 Shift
88 Like some triangles
90 Dam agcy.
91 Hockey's Lindros
92 Hollywood dive?
93 Ostracized one
94 Ready to spit
95 Caterpillar hairs
96 Via
97 Case workers: abbr.
101 Summer getaway, perhaps
102 School orgs.
103 Big letters in public broadcasting
106 Race car sponsor
107 Columbus, for one: abbr.
108 Christina's dad
109 Prelude to a hickey

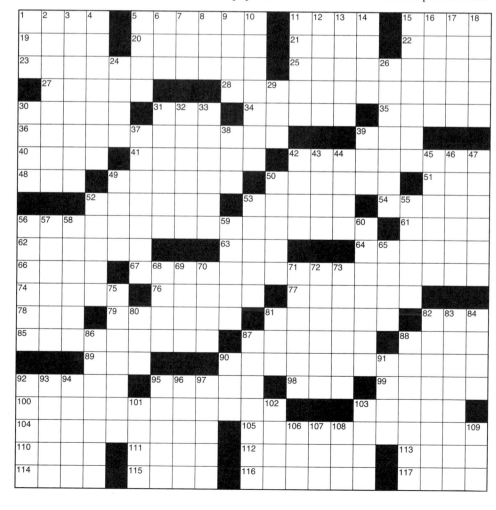

Simply Simpsons

In November 2008 the Fox Network aired an episode of "The Simpsons" called "Homer and Lisa Exchange Cross Words." In it, Lisa becomes hooked on crosswords, enters a crossword tournament and loses, only to find out afterward that Homer had bet heavily that she would indeed lose and as a result he won a boatload of cash. She instantly disowns him. To win her back, Homer spends the money on a special Sunday New York Times crossword, constructed by me and edited by Will Shortz, containing two apologies — one hidden in the grid's diagonal and one spelled out by the initial letters of all 144 clues. This puzzle actually appeared in the Times's Sunday magazine the day the episode aired, but since the apologies were hidden, the vast majority of solvers never noticed them until they watched the episode.

Will and I appear as cartoon versions of ourselves at the very end of the episode to explain the apologies to Lisa. (And now that I think of it, I'm still waiting for my share of Homer's winnings.)

When the idea for the Sunday puzzle tie-in was broached to Will and me by the episode's writer, Tim Long, we eventually agreed on a single idea, that the apologies should be hidden, that no one solving the puzzle initially should sense any connection to "The Simpsons," that the "reveal" should come on the show itself.

This left the other approach wide open for me. My regular weekly puzzle appears in about 50 papers every Sunday, so I still had a puzzle to make for my own markets, and this was a chance to make the opposite of a "hidden message" puzzle" — that is, a totally in-your-face "Simpsons" puzzle.

And this led to three rather amazing things about the show — amazing coincidences, really — all of which are in the puzzle. Just take note of 101, 127, and 130 Across. (A more detailed explanation appears on the puzzle's solution page.)

Oh, and one more thing. Now that you've read this book's 4-wd. and the pieces on Arthur Wynne and Kay (you did read them, right?), it does seem appropriate to close this 100th anniversary book with a puzzle about "The Simpsons." After all, Arthur Wynne had thousands of words to choose from when he made that first brain-teaser back in 1913. Who could have ever predicted that DOH would be one of them?

Here's to you, Puzzle That Started It All. Shine on, you crazy diamond.

—MR

NOTE: *Asterisks indicate clues that contain "Simpsons" characters as answers.*

ACROSS

1 Crossword-solving Simpson
5 Certain electrodes
13 Uris novel, "The ___"
16 Sock-in-the-gut grunt
19 "Holy moly!"
20 Prepares spuds, perhaps
21 "Adam and Eve ___!" (diner slang for two eggs on toast)
23 Bonds, for example *
25 Neck areas
26 "Good Night" girl
27 Lessen
28 A verb tense: abbr.
30 Collection of outlets?
32 Pointless weapons
34 Only black key in the "Simpsons" theme, if you play it in F major (see 127 Across)
38 1872 novel *
44 Crenshaw relative
45 Pound sound
46 Dodsworth's wife
47 "___ Ben Adhem"
49 JFK Library architect
50 1965 march site*
53 Outlaw
54 Took a header
55 "There ___ ..."
56 Solar-wind particle
57 Avian sounds
59 Bit of trail mix
60 Campaign, perhaps
65 Iowa's state tree
66 "Fur is dead" org.
69 Elvis features *
72 Kettle of fish
75 Electrician's word of meditation?
77 Harboring a thief, e.g.
79 Hotel waiter?
81 Works like a spider
86 Do roadwork
87 Pro ___
88 It has its limits
89 Passing fancy
90 Breakfast option *
95 Carrier letters
96 Poodle's name
97 Bane of youth
98 Like car glass
99 Sheep remarks
101 Archrivals of the Longhorns (with ampersand) *
105 Shenanigan
106 Theater lobby
107 ___-en-scene
108 "Hazel" co-star Don
110 WWI fighter plane
112 K.T. of country
117 Trailing ___ (evergreen shrub)
120 Born in Buenos Aires, perhaps *
124 Monkeys (with)
125 Taken, as a seat
126 Rainbow shapes
127 (Just so you know, the famous last notes of the "Simpsons" theme run diagonally up the grid from this corner to the upper right)
128 Turn blue?
129 Most run-down
130 Homer's imp son

DOWN

1 Site of a Samson slaughter
2 Noted lab assistant
3 "___ to you!"
4 Yemeni port
5 Australian grazer
6 Will Ferrell played one in a Christmas movie
7 "___ return"
8 Anything but that?
9 Henri's head
10 Record book suffix
11 Want to forget
12 More agile
13 Med. ctrs.
14 Ending to avoid?
15 Grammy-winning Al
16 Dolt
17 Away from
18 Knox and Dix: abbr.
22 Collars with folds
24 Shark-riding fish
29 Minnesota mining range
31 Catered event
32 Dutch cheese
33 Carlos of baseball
35 Place for a pin
36 Clear as ___
37 Astaire wear
38 "___ Apple"
39 Wrote out
40 Recently
41 Pinup's legs
42 Jets' home: abbr.
43 Colt's fans?: abbr.
44 Oceanfront unit, often
48 Happy hour site
51 Costello bio, "___ on First"
52 Years, to Caesar
54 Ersatz
57 Unibrowed Muppet
58 Spy tool, briefly
61 One little squeeze worth
62 Fighting Johnny
63 Grampa Simpson
64 Set shout
67 Chichi
68 Spa sighs
70 Naldi or Talbot
71 Hitch in plans
73 Veteran character actor Vito
74 South Carolina river
76 Secret society
78 Garbo et al.
80 Hopalong portrayer William et al.
81 Frogman's acronym
82 Certain Tuscan
83 Where ___ (*the* place to go)
84 Old military aux.
85 Sentence shortener, often
87 Screen door sound
90 Old German region, ___-Coburg
91 Rent-___
92 Young ___
93 It has a wet floor
94 Con victim
96 Like some gems
100 Keep raising, at an auction
102 An ___ detail
103 Donny ___
104 Tiny flies
106 "All That Jazz" man
109 Intense anger
110 Net Nanny target
111 Slugger David Ortiz's nickname, Big ___
113 Slangy attempt
114 Old Italian bread?
115 Boost: abbr.
116 Cartoonist Thomas
117 Justice Dept. org.
118 33 Down, for one
119 ASCAP rival
121 HDTV maker
122 Leaf-changing mo.
123 Summer hrs. in D.C.

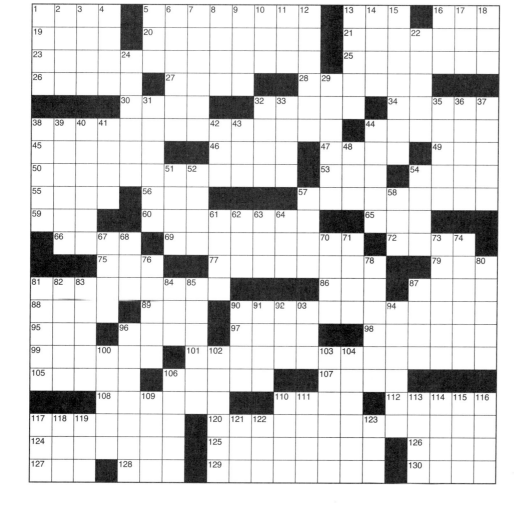

Crossword Puzzles

1 — Across-word Puzzle

```
MAIA  WINO  FLOR  SOSA
ABCWIDEWORLDOFSPORTS
ACHILDSGARDENOFVERSES
SHOE AMOS  AYN  STOW
HORROR   HIC   ANT
 FEMALECHROMOSOMES
SCAM ATALE EROO OATH
SHARECROPPERSSON ZITI
TERI HIPS  ELON LINEN
URI PIN  ASTON  LEER
BACHELOROFARTSDEGREES
AONE ARTOO  OAS  ALI
SATON ANTE  TWOS USER
UPUP ACCORDIONLESSONS
EARL SMOG MOREI ANNA
TREACHEROUSWATERS
 AES  TOA  ASFAST
GOAL CLU  TOLL READ
WILLIAMCARLOSWILLIAMS
TRAFFICCONTROLSYSTEM
SOFA RIPS ROSS  DOAS
```

2 — Repeat Business

```
TRUSSED PLEDGE DAKOTA
AIRHOLE RENOIR ELIXIR
OFFOFFBROADWAY JSTONE
STARE IPSO  SAME
 TWENTYTWENTYVISION
ISO VEAL BEIRUT DOT
GOB NIL AFORE HITME
OLLYOLLYOXENFREE CAPS
IDIOM ACTED MRRIGHT
NEGRI EXTOL TAIGA
GREENGREENGRASSOFHOME
 ALIST RAMPS FINAL
ANGELIC GENIC IGETA
DIRE BAABAABLACKSHEEP
ATONE SALTY HAH YRS
PRO VELCRO JEAN ESE
TOMTOMTHEPIPERSSON
 ELMS NUNS SINAI
OCTAVE NEVERNEVERLAND
TEASET AVERSE ANILINE
TOREST BAXTER CSCALES
```

3 — Snacks on a Plane

```
ADOLFO  FRET MALDEMER
SOBEIT CREDO ILLUSIVE
PRETZELVANIA STARTLES
SOYUZ OINKS ARENA ENT
 PERM COOKIEROBERTS
ALI DEPP NORA SLA
RENE NORSK NEDS ESSEN
PEANUTCOLADA SAM ELIA
ADDONS CUBE  SADSONG
SECS TENONS THRU WES
CHEESEGOTTAHAVEIT
ATL AXED MURRAY NOAH
TRIPLET RUIN ANNLEE
MINI CSI BETTYCRACKER
SMELT ENCL SHOAL EELS
 AWE SAAB UVEA RST
MUFFINTHEBALL ESSO
UNO SCORN NAOMI TRACT
SHORTONE RAISINTHEBAR
TITTERED ANNEX AMOUSE
SPEEDERS MAES GASTAX
```

4 — Cliché Combos

```
COLI DOUG ASOF  FAQS
ABUNDANTLYCLEAR ABUT
UNVARNISHEDTRUTH DJIA
PHINEAS ANS VIOL ELY
SEAN  RND FARM ACCTS
EAT CAPITALIDEA ROT
TRE LION ALA  FRYPAN
 WENTSWIMMINGLY ODE
SIFT EEL ROUES VOW
GODS LIAM PRE SENT
MORE RANKAMATEUR TRIS
ADEN EXO DANA GETS
GIL ATLAS ICY PLAY
IVY BREAKNECKSPEED
CALMLY EOS ACRE PAL
ABU PRINCELYSUM ILE
PICAS AONE VEE SOLE
INK HALO YEN RESCUER
NAIL GOTALONGFAMOUSLY
ZINE EMINENTLYDOABLE
ARGO ANTI SEIS PAYS
```

5 — George Steinbrenner For President

```
JAIL EARNIT BEACH
FROMLEFTFIELD UNCLE
THEBIGLEAGUES LTTRAGG
SIC EAU RAT OGRE VOL
ZAP TEA ESAU ADAYTO
TOMATO SHORTSTOP RHOS
IMETA TIU RIPS CRIBS
MELONS OTT ADESTE TAY
 UNDERHANDED WYATT
JOT ESL EGO ABA LEFT
APHID SCREWBALL SEROW
MERL PEA IRE AFT SRO
NOLIE RUNNINGHARD
SSW FRUTTI NEA BOOGIE
ITSAS TRIG GAL DERBY
MAAM TOUCHBASE SERENE
INCASH NATO SAL STS
ACU PEEK YDS REM CAM
NERDIER PLAYEDCATCHUP
 VOLVO YANKEESVSREDS
ESTES EIDERS ETON
```

6 — Triple Doubles

```
BOTTOM RFD  TMS TAU
AVEENO CALEB BOOTCAMP
TOLLFREECALL AGREESON
 LITTLEGREENAPPLES
MEG RIAL INST HIE
ABODES GOODQUEENBESS
RODE ESSEN  ADT VEE
KLIEG HARM EGOS OCEAN
JIMMYKIMMELLIVE INNS
 SPIN AARE FIASCO
SOP SLEEPTILLNOON OER
ARROYO RUIN ROBO
STET COFFEETABLEBOOK
HEFTS HOFF GOBI DELHI
AGA LEI GRETA SEAN
YABBADABBADOO IHEARD
 ALI RUNE OHME NEA
ABBOTTANDCOSTELLO
BLUEMOON MEETTHEMUMMY
HOLLERAT ENNIO SETTEE
OWL DST TOR STANDS
```

7 — One Fine Day at the Animal Salon

```
MINORS   ACLU    JEER    OVA
URANIA   NOEND   AXLE    SIR
COMEONINDEER     PUISSANT
KNEW  KNEE   QATAR   TOKYO
      IRAQ   GUYINBUFFALO  NOT
ERASE    UNCLASP
SUCHAWEASEL      THEREBEL
ATM   RESCAN   KIROV   RENO
USES  ATL   SUTURED   RIB
      CURS   JACKALANDHYDE
      BRAG   RETALLY   AILS
YOURHARETODAY    RAYS
URN   STEVENS   AHS   SLUG
LETS  REESE   DILATE   ONA
EDONEILL   TOTAPIRABIT
      ASA   TSETSES   ILOVE
ALITTLEMOOSE     ORCA
DENCH  MEANT   LIDO   SETS
LATHERED   YAKETYYAKYAK
IVE   TORE   STINT   CIARDI
BEL   ENYA   ENZO   ERNEST
```

8 — A-I-A-I-Oh!

```
       SCARE   ATMS   CEST
       RAISINGCAIN   AXIOM
       HITTHECAMPAIGNTRAIL
LUC   YEN   SEE   POI   STAID
ELKE   ZAP   LEONA   MAY
MAINSAIL   LAISSEZFAIRE
   LIB   PEERS   SOUL
JAIALAI   VICTIM   RONDO
ACTIV   GSA   DAIRYMAID
YES   ITOO   PALERMO   APED
   PORTRAITPAINTER
EACH   ATTUNES   LOOM   AXE
SNAILMAIL   CUT   EGLIN
PABLO   EDWARD   AIRRAID
   INKS   AVOID   FIE
TAIPEITAIWAN   JAILBAIT
IBM   MAZDA   ASP   ELSA
LETBE   MOL   FLU   AHA   LOX
THEREIVESAIDITAGAIN
   ELIAN   RETAILCHAIN
   AQUA   STEM   SHARD
```

9 — Dog Breeds I'd Like To See

```
MCII   AURA   FLUNKS   MCQ
ARNOLDPOMERANIAN   TAU
CINNAMONRAISINBEAGLE
   SITIN   TEST   URGES
TVA   ACR   EYED   OLDE
WISENHEIMARANER   STAC
INTO   ZIP   OPRAH   EDA
SCHNOOZER   MIDAIREDALE
TEE   MRI   STOMA   NEMESIS
   NANO   HEFTS   LENA
SPEKINGESE   RATTWEILER
PAAR   DEFOE   LAIT
ENROOTS   COREA   INC   TOA
WELCHSCORGI   WELKHOUND
ERA   MEUSE   AOK   PLEA
RAPS   BOTTOMLESSSPITZ
   UPSA   HMOS   NIT   POE
   DOESA   ODIE   EASED
JERRYSPRINGERSPANIEL
AMY   CHOCOLATEMALTESE
BOX   HADANY   ABET   STEW
```

10 — Some People Are Never Satisfied

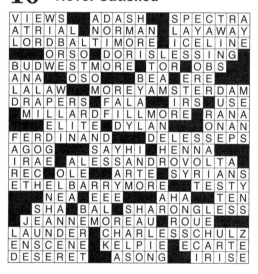

```
VIEWS   ADASH   SPECTRA
ATRIAL   NORMAN   LAYAWAY
LORDBALTIMORE   ICELINE
   ORSO   DORISLESSING
BUDWESTMORE   TOR   OBS
ANA   OSO   BEA   ERE
LALAW   MOREYAMSTERDAM
DRAPERS   FALA   IRS   USE
MILLARDFILLMORE   RANA
ELITE   DYLAN   ONAN
FERDINAND   DELESSEPS
AGOG   SAYHI   HENNA
IRAE   ALESSANDROVOLTA
REC   OLE   ARTE   SYRIANS
ETHELBARRYMORE   TESTY
NEA   EEE   AHA   TEN
SHA   BAL   SHARONGLESS
JEANNEMOREAU   ROUE
LAUNDER   CHARLESSCHULZ
ENSCENE   KELPIE   ECARTE
DESERET   ASONG   IRISE
```

11 — Are You Ready for Some Foodball?

```
CASPAR   BABBLE   SLUSH
MORAINE   AGORAS   PICTO
PILINGON   DESERT   IGLOO
ALL   DEUT   SECONDHALF
BEATTHESPREAD   POET
ARROYOS   LIP   SUPERBOWL
APR   RAPID   SEL   OREO
PRESFASON   CURED   EXALT
RUNTO   EDDA   MED   TRENDS
ANDY   PTA   FAME   THIS
YES   GAINOFFIFTEEN   SPA
LAWN   MITE   RAM   SOAR
POSITS   TAX   STEM   STUCK
SALVE   PINES   HASHMARKS
SHUI   ORE   DOSED   OUT
TURNOVERS   FEW   ASSUAGE
GRIM   CATCHOFTHEDAY
POUREDITON   UOFA   MGR
ELSOL   SITTER   OVERTIME
NINOS   ENTIRE   LOWFARE
ANAME   SASSED   DREDGE
```

12 — Old Paint

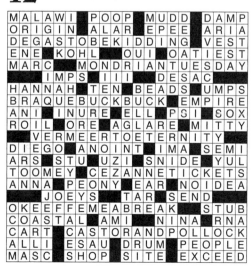

```
MALAWI   POOP   MUDD   DAMP
ORIGIN   ALAR   EPEE   ARIA
DEGASTOBEKIDDING   VEST
ENE   KOHL   OUI   OATIEST
MARC   MONDRIANTUESDAY
   IMPS   III   DESAC
HANNAH   TEN   BEADS   UMPS
BRAQUEBUCKBUCK   EMPIRE
ANI   INURE   ELL   PSI   SOX
ROIL   ORE   AGLARE   MITTY
VERMEERTOETERNITY
DIEGO   ANOINT   IMA   SEMI
ARS   STU   UZI   SNIDE   YUL
TOOMEY   CEZANNETICKETS
ANNA   PEONY   EAR   NOIDEA
   JOEYS   TAR   SEND
OKEEFFEMEABREAK   STUB
COASTAL   AMI   NINA   RNA
CART   CASTORANDPOLLOCK
ALLI   ESAU   DRUM   PEOPLE
MASC   SHOP   SITE   EXCEED
```

13 Pirates!

```
JOSE   MGS   DTS   FAT
AFARM GORY LOOT SOHOT
INDIA LRON UNAU AGAME
LOOKSDAGGERSAT BIGBEN
    ERA   OTT   EEL
 PAM AYN MAY CFL OMS
ISLAND  KID TOT SCOUT
AHERO DJIA RSA MUTINY
CARIBBEAN SEAS YEARNS
TWO LWOW CARTES DAY
   BEAR BEADS LTDS
 GIL NOSIER  HEIR TET
URSULA PEGS BUCCANEER
BEARDS ARS KANT KOREA
SCATS DRS KEG FEARED
OCS RES LAY AIR AYE
    EVE CUR ETA
SKULLS CUTLASSSUPREME
BASIL FORE LEOS ROGER
ATSEA LASS EXPO SPAIN
ERS ATE SYS ELMO
```

The six diagonally "buried" items are GOLD, DOUBLOONS, JEWELS, PIECES OF EIGHT, SILVER and PEARLS.

14 Hard-To-Do Songs

```
FIBER OLEG   APPT FIT
ORATE RELIVE HALO ICH
CATCHAFALLINGSTAR REX
IQS EROS LEDA SYSTEM
 MAKETHEWORLDGOAWAY
ATTARS ITS ORO JAKE
FORI MSGT SPRYLY TEA
FLYMETOTHEMOON FAKERS
ELO MOMA UNPEG WORST
CENSUS GUMBOS EAST
TREE CRYMEARIVER TARA
 THAI BERATE TOOLED
STRIA PARKA SHIN IDO
KOONTZ WALKONTHEOCEAN
IRS HERESY CASH ANTI
PEEK POL SCI RINSES
 SAVEUPALLYOURTEARS
DINNER IVAR ARGO WHO
COL CLIMBEVRYMOUNTAIN
URL LINE SEEMED EARLY
ESE ENGR DARE DETOX
```

15 Screen Gem

```
GAEL ICBM MEL APIANS
OGEE BRAY AGAR BANJOS
WARS MADD CATA ERMINE
ITIS ZEE BLIP SEGO
THEONLYGAMEINTOWN
HARRYO GROTTO HAI APE
MWF THESANDPIPER
BRAE ERST MOS KERR
RAINTREECOUNTY LEXUS
AMOK ALAR LIE MME
FATHERSLITTLEDIVIDEND
LEO MIR HOLM ELOI
BALKS APLACEINTHESUN
AQUI OIL RENE IRAN
BUTTERFIELD8 RAM
YAZ VAN AURORA COLONS
ALITTLENIGHTMUSIC
MEADE OWLS CHE NIKE
VORTEX BEAD HALF GRIN
ANGORA ELBE ISLE SITE
TAOISM LYN ETON SAS
```

The large chunky black squares around the diagram's perimeter spell out the word LIZ four times.

16 Paul's Puzzle

```
SFLA ROYALIST ILLS
AREAS HEADACHE MEETS
WECANWORKITOUT DATUM
SET OAS MIN DOSIDO
RUFUS GMEN PROW TIC
HERETHERE HITON BOK
DIET TAO DUPED DEBS
ANDEVERYWHERE AWE
 AXE EAR ADORNED
SHARP ASALAMB REEVE
YOURMOTHERSHOULDKNOW
ELEMI MALTOSE EASEL
PEDANTS LIU SAG
NTH HELTERSKELTER
MAGI EMERY NUT AIRE
ARE BORES YESTERDAY
PCT ENID SCAD RAKES
LATETE BAA SIS PUP
EDICT THENIGHTBEFORE
SINCE DIATRIBE SHOES
AGER SCRANTON ALSO
```

17 I Now Pronounce You ... Differently

```
ARID OHMS ASA OILMEN
MENACHEMBEGIN ALREADY
BERKEBREATHED RESERVE
IKE LEA CAV III SKAT
TEL LEM SETBACK MRS
GARYOLDMAN WES APED
ALEE ASTRO COX CHASMS
IMADAM ISAAC PURSUE
TAT MICHAELLANDON INE
DONEE LEROI ANECK
EAU ALI JOB TSP HRH
ASNEW ENFEU ICALL
TAN ROBERTREDFORD LIE
WIRIER ITSME TSGARP
OMEGAS KEY ACTSO OBOE
OINK GUZ JOEYFATONE
URN SPAREME REB THU
SAKI OUT AVE APR RHO
ELINORS PRINCERAINIER
TENTOES VLADIMIRPUTIN
OSGOOD TON DUSK NERO
```

18 Where Am I?

```
CPOS OVAL UTAH OTIS
ALVA ROBE GALAS SUDAN
BAER BROOMHILDA STOLE
CRAG TUNAS WALL UNIX
TACHOMETER BEREA STET
ATA TAX VIE ORCA TRU
TEMPOS JOINTOWNERSHIP
IDEAS NUNNERY ORIBI
YEHUDI PALS TANDY
THEAUDACITY WASH KEA
POUR RISEN EDICT ASAP
BAG KLEE PARISHILTON
STERN SAIL CHERIE
QUITS BEEGEES KILTS
COUNTYOURCARDS GENIAL
ARA SPUR EPA CAN SKI
RIND ELSAS DEVASTATED
TOTO SMUG SENOR OLEO
ELIZA ALIENATION INFO
DETER NARCO ELLA BIFF
SYNC SLOW RASP INST
```

19 Sorry, Wrong Letter! (6)

20 Tri-V-ial Pursuit

21 Like, Totally Jazzed

```
TRIB SANTA FREDA  ASTA
RENO ARIAS ABLER  UNIX
ITSALLINTHERIFFS  DAME
PIU  HAZE  CASS  RERIP
UNLOAD BASH PANE   CRY
PATHS BORNTOBLUES  ROE
   TARARA ROAD   UDALL
ATMO ELEVS TLC  IMACOP
THEBASSMENT    TEANECK
BOLERO ROOF  BLT  ELAN
ASL BLOWYOURNOTES  ELO
YEOW DUH TRIO    RAMBLE
  WIRETAP NATKINGCOOL
REDFIR TEL  RAISE  APTS
ORRIN  EIRE    BELTED
AMA SAXFIFTHAVE  ROUST
RAM ELIS  TIED  ROOMIE
  AUDIT  ROMA SKID  LEN
BUTT GROOVERCLEVELAND
ASIA NORSE YOURE  DUNE
MACH SWEAR EXERT  STAR
```

22 Pun Clearance

```
ARTFORM  ASTA  HOMONYM
LEARNERS PHIL  ADAPTED
APRIAMSUSPECT  BERTHAS
  STAB  RULE   DELI
  REMEMBERTHEALAMODE
BIN TAXI    ROBS  CIDER
OMEN HAST PESO   HADME
YOUOWEMEONEKENOBI  SAC
DARTERS POP   AXE  CENT
SNORT   PRESCIENTAND
  SAW  ISLA  TARN  RRS
  ACCOUNTEDFOR   APAGE
ALIE ACU   AIR  AMMETER
SEE GRAFTONCORRUPTION
CANOE  FRUG TAGS  SODS
OSCAR  PIES   POTS  NET
THEFORDEXTRADITION
  NAIR   ALOE    SAAB
JAYBIRD MALLARDJUSTED
GROOMED OSLO  SERRATED
SENSORY WHYY   PRELATE
```

23 It's Not What It Looks Like

24 Eat, Drink, and Be Merry

25 — Eat, Drink, and Be Murray

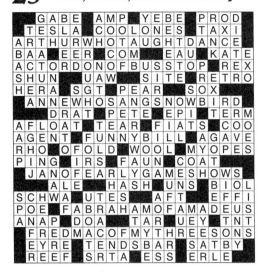

```
GABE  AMP  YEBE  PROD
TESLA COOLONES  TAXI
ARTHURWHOTAUGHTDANCE
BAA EER COM EAU KATE
ACTORDONOFBUSSTOP REX
SHUN UAW SITE RETRO
HERA SGT PEAR SOX
ANNEWHOSANGSNOWBIRD
DRAT PETE EPI TERM
AFLOAT TEAR FIATS COO
AGENT FUNNYBILL AGAVE
RHO OFOLD WOOL MYOPES
PING IRS FAUN COAT
JANOFEARLYGAMESHOWS
ALE HASH UNS BIOL
SCHWA UTES AFT EFFI
POE FABRAHAMOFAMADEUS
ANAP DOA TAR UEY TNT
FREDMACOFMYTHREESONS
EYRE TENDSBAR SATBY
REEF SRTA ESS ERLE
```

26 — Apply Directly to Your (___)

```
WORM WEBS STAB OTTO
IMAC SABOT BOOLA WHIM
TOUCHEDBYANANGEL LUGE
HOLLERS TROD IVES MEG
ONA DORSALVERTEBRA
LETUSPRAY NOEL AMA
ACID HAH ATKA STORKS
MOM GLOBALMARKETING
ALEWIFE CAKE MOI EDIT
SERENE FOCI SPELL ETS
SCREAMINGEAGLES
OFT ARACE GALS EVADER
CLAW OSE FARM STIMULI
HALIBUTTERIYAKI NEG
SPICES GEMS ELF INME
ACE SHOE INTURMOIL
DISAPPOINTMENT RAH
ASH SENT IOTA FINALES
RUIN ENORMOUSSEEDPODS
EZRA RENEE DEARS PLOT
DUET STEP ECON YAMS
```

27 — A Bunch of Two-Timing Name-Droppers

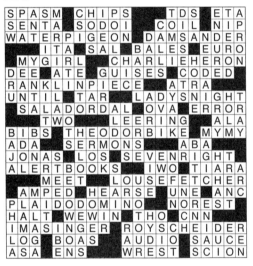

```
SPASM CHIPS TDS ETA
SENTA SODOI COIL NIP
WATERPIGEON DAMSANDER
ITA SAL BALES EURO
MYGIRL CHARLIEHERON
DEE ATE GUISES CODED
RANKLINPIECE ATRA
UNTIL TAR LADYSNIGHT
SALADORDAL OVA ERROR
TWO LEERING ALA
BIBS THEODORBIKE MYMY
ADA SERMONS ABA
JONAS LOS SEVENRIGHT
ALERTBOOKS IWO TIARA
MEET LOUSEFETCHER
AMPED HEARSE UNE ANC
PLAIDODOMINO NOREST
HALT WEWIN THO CNN
IMASINGER ROYSCHEIDER
LOG BOAS AUDIO SAUCE
ASA ENS WREST SCION
```

28 — Deal!

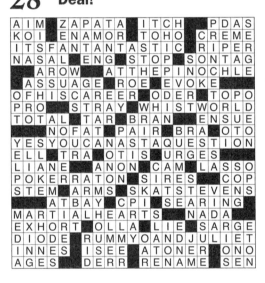

```
AIM ZAPATA ITCH PDAS
KOI ENAMOR TOHO CREME
ITSFANTANTASTIC RIPER
NASAL ENG STOP SONTAG
AROW ATTHEPINOCHLE
ASSUAGE ROE EVOKE
OFHISCAREER ODER TOPO
PRO STRAY WHISTWORLD
TOTAL TAR BRAN ENSUE
NOFAT PAIR BRA OTO
YESYOUCANASTAQUESTION
ELL TRA OTIS URGES
LIANE ANON CAM LASSO
POKERRATON SIRES COP
STEM ARMS SKATSTEVENS
ATBAY CPI SEARING
MARTIALHEARTS NADA
EXHORT OLLA LIE SARGE
DIODE RUMMYOANDJULIET
INNES ISEE ATONER ONO
AGES DERR RENAME SEN
```

29 — Basket of Goodies

```
GNASH GEM ABR
JOUSTER ORLY GEOM
ARTHURHONMER ENDALL
KASEM DONT CAFETERIA
FLO AR THATSO HOTLY
CANSECO COEDS IFA ILA
PRON PAWS LOM NIN
ELSA INCASH ROSS CHP
LOCH NIA TIEON SIDEUP
AVRIL ERR TRUE INSITU
TEA EASTEREGGROLL DIE
EMMETT OPAH HEF ABOAR
DEBTTO NONOS EDT RENT
TLC NAST UPFLOW ORSO
REE PER ISAT LOBO
AND IDO ODETS LOOMYOO
IDEAL MARILU SSW EON
SEGREGATE ALEC LEANS
ARGOSY SCHWARZENOER
SOIR EARN BARRELS
MNO ARE READS
```

30 — A Student of the '60s

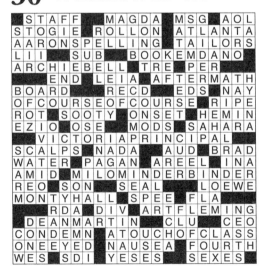

```
STAFF MAGDA MSG AOL
STOGIE ROLLON ATLANTA
AARONSPELLING TAILORS
LII SUB BOOKEMDANO
ARCHIEBELL TRE PER
END LEIA AFTERMATH
BOARD RECD EDS NAY
OFCOURSEOFCOURSE RIPE
ROT SOOTY ONSET HEMIN
EZIO OSE MODS SAHARA
VICTORIAPRINCIPAL
SCALPS NADA AUD BRAD
WATER PAGAN AREEL INA
AMID MILOMINDERBINDER
REO SON SEAL LOEWE
MONTYHALL SPEE FLA
RDA DIV ARTFLEMING
DEANMARTIN CLU CEO
CONDEMN ATOUCHOFCLASS
ONEEYED NAUSEA FOURTH
WES SDI YESES SEXES
```

31 Halloween Party Checklist

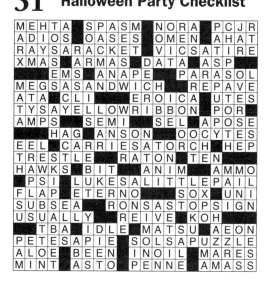

```
M E H T A  S P A S M  N O R A  P C J R
A D I O S  O A S E S  O M E N  A H A T
R A Y S A R A C K E T  V I C S A T I R E
X M A S  A R M A S  D A T A  A S P
     E M S  A N A P E  P A R A S O L
M E G S A S A N D W I C H  R E P A V E
A T A  C L I  E R O I C A  U T E S
T Y S A Y E L L O W R I B B O N  P O R
A M P S  S E M I  S E L  A P O S E
   H A G  A N S O N  O O C Y T E S
E E L  C A R R I E S A T O R C H  H E P
T R E S T L E  R A T O N  T E N
H A W K S  B I T  A N I M  A M M O
  P S I  L U K E S A L I T T L E P A I L
F L A P  E T E R N O  S O X  U N I
S U B S E A  R O N S A S T O P S I G N
U S U A L L Y  R E I V E  K O H
   T B A  I D L E  M A T S U  A E O N
P E T E S A P I E  S O L S A P U Z Z L E
A L O E  B E E N  I N O I L  M A R E S
M I N T  A S T O  P E N N E  A M A S S
```

32 Gag Me with a Spoonerism

```
S L O  D A L Y  E S P N  A P O P
Q U I  O R D O  L A S E R  C L A R A
C A L  W A L K I N G Y O U R H A R E S
M U S T N T  E N I A C  F O O T  F T S
  P A K  A L U N C H O F B O O Z E R S
S M I L E A T  R O E  F L O  I R O N
B E L L Y J E A N S  D O E  Y A P
A L L Y  A A R  S O L  M I L I T I A
  H U M M I N G A N D P L E A T I N G
A L O E  E R T E  A L L  E U R
B U S Y C H E W I N G T H E D O O R S
A R C  O A T  M E A N  W I S E
B A C K T O T H E M A L T S I G N S
C M I N O R S  X E R  O S U  T S A R
  U P S  C P R  W A I T F O R T H E
R I O T  P L O  C A T  O F P A R I S
O T H E R D R E W T O S H O P  E K E
D E L  A R A N  H O H O S  I N H A L E
M O N K E Y C H I L D S A L S A  K I X
S O N E S  H O S E A  K A L I  E V E
  K E D S  W I R Y  A G E R  R E C
```

33 Trinonyms

```
S A M E  C A M P S  C R A G S  M A Y A
A P E X  A B O U T  L I B R A  O P E D
F E L T  B U N N Y R A B B I T  P I L L
A M O  W I C K  L E M  A S I A  E L I
R A T F I N K  D E B U G  T A X I C A B
I N T U N E  S O D A P O P  T E N E T S
   M O T I L E  G I S E L E
Z O N E  F O R E F R O N T  Z A P S
I D A  D E E M  V I A  E R I C  Q U A
N E V  O L E O M A R G A R I N E  U R I
C R Y S T A L  O D E T S  P U L S A R S
  W E T  P R E D A T E  R E T
T A P E R E C O R D  G E T O N B O A R D
A R E A  P R O  R E S  P R O A
K I T T Y C A T  A T M  S U M T O T A L
E A S I E R  S H A R I  I S F I N E
   T H E D E P A R T M E N T O F
A G O  E R N O  S P E E  Q U I
R E D U N D A N C Y  D E P A R T M E N T
C N O T E  N U K E  E X I T  W A I T E
S T R A W  K I S S  B Y E S  A X I O M
```

34 The First-Name Game

```
B A N A N A  G O G O  W A S B A D
A D O N I S  R E L I C S  R A P T U R E
G L O T T I S K N I G H T  O F S O R T S
S E N O R  P O R O U S P A S T E R N A K
  R E N A M E  E S E  M T S  M A S
   S T I L T  S U M O  C Y D
U H F  E N T R E E S E G O V I A  E G O
B A L A  S E N S U A L  O N A B E T
E R A S E D  E S S E  I M A N  S T A T
R A T T L E S  A Z T E C S  C I P R O
  S T O I C A L L Y C A R M I C H A E L
U S E R S  C A E S A R  S H A T T E R
N E R I  A S O F  N O D S  G R I E V E
D R Y A D S  T R A I N T O  C R E D
O S O  J U M P B A L L J O N E S  S R O
  C B S  O L E G  P E C A N
R O E  A W E  F A V  S O L O N G
C O N D O L E A S E R R I C E  A M O O N
R U N O V E R  C L E M E N C Y M O O R E
A T O N E R S  I M D O W N  M I S S E S
W E R E N T  O A R S  A S S E N T
```

35 Rule Breaker

```
C L A S S I F I E D A D V E R T I S I N G
E U R O  N  F E R M I U M  H  I S E E
L L C  S T S  L I B R E  S I G  M R T
E L  S T E W S  P I E  S E R U M  O T
B  W H E R E T O  V  A M A D E U S  I
R E C O N N A I S S A N C E M I S S I O N
I  S E N A T E S  L  T A I N T E D  G
T V  S I T E S  P C W  R E F E R  J O
Y A M  S I R  B E N E S  R A D  F A N
E M I T  O  N O T T R U E  N  R A Y E
N O T H A N K Y O U  E I G H T B A L L S
D O R Y  A  E R N E S T O  R  G L E E
O S E  T L C  S I D E S  D Y E  S N L
R E  R E D A S  A S T  M E D A L  O F
S  S A L A B L E  U  M I L I T I A  I
E D U C A T I O N A L T E L E V I S I O N
M  R E V E N G E  L  R E T I N A L  S
E E  R I L E S  T I M  R E S T S  O H
N R C  V I T  J A V A N  R I O  U P A
T I L L  N  G O T A J O B  O  A S A P
S Q U A R E P E G I N A R O U N D H O L E
```

36 Sounds from the Past

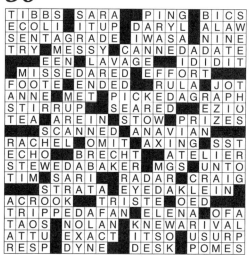

```
T I B B S  S A R A  P I N G  B I C S
E C O L I  I T U P  D A R Y L  A L A W
S E N T A G R A D E  I W A S A  N I N E
T R Y  M E S S Y  C A N N E D A D A T E
   E E N  L A V A G E  I D I D I T
   M I S S E D A R E D  E F F O R T
F O O T E  E N D E D  R U L A  J O T
A N N E  M E T  P I C K E D A G R A P H
S T I R R U P  S E A R E D  E Z I O
T E A  A R E I N  S T O W  P R I Z E S
   S C A N N E D  A N A V I A N
R A C H E L  O M I T  A X I N G  S S T
E C H O  B R E C H T  A T E L I E R
S T E W E D A B A K E R  M G S  U N T O
T I M  S A R I  R A D A R  C R A I G
   S T R A T A  E Y E D A K L E I N
A C R O O K  T R I S T E  O E D
T R I P P E D A F A N  E L E N A  O F A
T A O S  N O L A N  K N E W A R I V A L
A T T U  E X A C T  I T S O  U S U R P
R E S P  D Y N E  D E S K  P O M E S
```

37 Rock 'n' Bull Story

```
. A L P O . H E A R . O A F S . J I M I
. D O I T . B A B A . F R A C T U R E D
J U N E F O R A Y . F A I R Y T A L E S
. U R I . C O P S . L A S T . B A T .
T H E P I C A Y U N E . E S P . I T A L Y
O A R S . H I E S . N E W . P H N O .
P G A . E R A . I N T E L L I G E N C E
O A T E S . S S N . A L O E S . R O A N
F R O S T B I T E F A L L S . D R O V E
. C O R D . M R X . I B L E . K I M .
S A E . W I L L I A M C O N R A D . S L Y
T U X . I G E T . E R N . A D U E .
A D E P T . G I D N E Y A N D C L O Y D
M I R A . S P O R E . M X L . T I M O R
P O T T S Y L V A N I A . L U V . A D O
. T U N A . T S A . A I N T . S H E L .
C A B I N . N N E . M R K N O W I T A L L
A T A . D U T Y . F A U N . O N O .
W O S S A M O T T A . B I L L S C O T T
. M R P E A B O D Y . I F S O . A G A R
. S A Y S . E L S E . N E D S . S E X Y
```

38 Floaters

```
W A N T . J A M B S . R T E . D E Y S .
S H A H . O C E A N . C O L D . A L O I S
W A V E S H E L L O . M O S C O W M U L E
. F I N D S L O O P H O L E S . W E E
A S W A R M . S T L . A L I D . S I N S
B U S T S I N . S O A R . Y A L T A
E N G . L E A . R E D O R Y E L L O W
S K I F F L E B A N D S . F E A S T
. L O O S . E T E . I S P Y . O S L O
E B E R . A L A M P U N T O M Y F E E T
A X E . C S T . R E A P S . T E A . R O T
S E R V E T W O M A S T E R S . L A O S
A C T I . R I P S . O R E . S I F T
A T I L T . C A N T A N K E R O U S
D I S C I P L I N E R . R B I . N N E
E L T O N . A E O N . A P A T I T E
B L E M . D A L I . M O A . A L A N O N
A W E . B E F O R E A N D A F T E R
T I P P E C A N O E . W A T E R C R A F T
E L L E N . N E B R . A L I T O . E V E R
. L Y R E . R I O . R E P E L . D E W Y
```

The hidden sailing vessels are SHELL, SCOW, SLOOP, DORY, SKIFF, PUNT, TWO-MASTER, TANKER, LINER, FORE-AND-AFTER, CANOE, and RAFT.

39 The Wright Frame of Mind

```
B U M S O U T . M O T I O N S . P E L T S
O N E A R T H . I N A T R E E . O P A R T
L I M I T E R . D E L I G H T . L O V E R
S T E N S . E C O L E S . S K Y D I V E
H I N T . M E A R A . A R C H I M E D E S
O N T . M E S S I N A . A H O L E . A S S
I G O T A J O B . E M A N A T O R S
. A R O M A S . E M I T . B I G R A M
I N A F I R E H Y D R A N T F A C T O R Y
N E S T E A . S O I T . E A R . S O D
S W I S S . B U T I C O U L D . C Y C L E
A L E . O O P . D A R T . A R E O L A
N E V E R P A R K A N Y W H E R E N E A R
E Y E L E T . I N R I . O U T L E T
. S T I N G I E S T . T H E P L A C E
A B O . A M A H S . M A R T E N S . S O W
P Y R A C A N T H A . C H O R E . D A T E
P R I C K L E . R O T I N I . A U B E R
O N E A L . T H I A M I N . Z I P C O D E
S E N S E . T A N G E L O . E L E A N O R
E S T E S . E S S E N E S . D E X T E R S
```

40 Zilch! Nada!

```
T O M . B A C H . C O D E . M I G .
O N O . A G R A . E C O N O . I N O N
I T S A B O U T N O T H I N G . S T O U T
T I T L E . C E E . A D E E D O O D A H
. M E A . I D A H O . S I N E . O F N O
E L S E M A T T E R S . D U B S . O C S
. R E L O . R E A T A S . L O R E
S T O P A T . B E L O W . H A H .
H I R E S . M O O G S . I N C O M M O N
A B A S E . A P N O E A . O R U S . M O H
W I N O . I R E N E . B I T E R . F E T A
L A G . I N C R . S A S S E S . A L L O R
L E S S T H A N . M O L D S . T I E U P
. O I L . A N I L E . N E X T T O
D O W N . L E M E N U . T H E A .
G U N . G A I A . B U T T H E T R U T H
A B E S . P S S T . S E M I S . R O O
T O S N E E Z E A T . A N T . B A H T S
S I L E X . T O L E R A N C E P O L I C Y
. S I R E . N O T C H . U R S A . D A N
. P D S . N E S S . T S A R . E R E
```

41 Something in Common

```
S E N S E D . R A M . G U M . C A T
K L U T Z E S . M A M A . U H U H . B I O
A S T A I R E . O V E R F I F T Y A S S N
. C O M P L A I N C O N S T A N T L Y
O M S K . A T E . O W E . N A V E S
F A M E D L A W M A N . L A M E N T
A N O D E . O T O O . E M I . R A T
G I G . R O B I N W I L L I A M S R O L E
E A S T . W O N . O R G A N D Y . O M E N
. H A L O E S . S A S H . P L E A S
A N G E L S P R O P . S T E E P S L O P E
W O R D S . T H O R . A R C H I E
A B O O . C A L I P E R . I R E . D A L E
S L I G H T L Y O U T O F T U N E . B A Y
H E N . O R E . P A A R . S C O P E
. U P S E T S . G R O U N D C O V E R
A N I S E . O I L . S E A . E E L S
N O T E D C H O R E O G R A P H E R
S T A R T R E K S P E E D . A L L C A P S
E S L . O A S T . E D N A . L I K E M A D
L O Y . M A O . R S T . A S S A Y S
```

The words, which appear in the clues in alphabetical order, are AARP, CARP, EARP, GARP, HARP, SCARP, SHARP, TARP, THARP, and WARP.

42 Connections

```
T O F U . E L S . L E A P T . B O A R S
O P E R A . X O O . A D L A I . I N L E T
W I L L - O - T H E - W I S P . T A L I A
N E T . R O M . O L D . S T I R . D - N Y
. D O N A T . M I S T Y . O M A N
S U N D A Y - G O - T O - M E E T I N G
C E R A . O B I . D U F F S . L E G A L
O T C . M O R A V I A N . A G E . H I E
H - H O U R . R E T . S B C . N E S T L E
A T I P T O E . H U M . L E T S G O
N O N - U . S H O P - M A D E . G - M E N
. E A R L A P . F E H . T H E S A M E
B E A D L E . N E S . I B M . E R O I C A
A L P . O A K . A I R L I N E S . D E R
H A R T S . M Y F U N . A M O . B E E S
T H E A T E R - I N - T H E - R O U N D
. S N A G . P L A S H . O F A N Y
T V - G . O P A L . T E A . A M E . X E S
O A S E S . U N - L O O K - U P - A B L E
A N K L E . S K I E R . I L L . A D O B E
D E I O N . S Y N G E . N Y T . E X A M
```

Early Puzzles

43 Marquees After the Storm

```
OCCULT  PEA  POGO
CHOREA  SANDPAPER
LICEINWONDERLAND
RONA  DAFT  AERIE
ICC  NTEST  HAMSTER
OKLAHOMACRUD
IMLOST  ARMS  PAM
ALPO  UNTIEMAME
NAPLES  MRT  TWOTON
THEESTMAN  THOU
ERR  SEAM  CALAIS
AYAKATOXFORD
REMAILS  ASIDE  FER
URALS  ARCS  OGPU
LOCALBOYMAKESGOO
ESOTERICA  ETHERS
RENE  ALE  THEEYE
```

44 On the Golden Gate

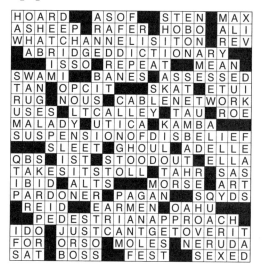

```
HOARD  ASOF  STEN  MAX
ASHEEP  RAFER  HOBO  ALI
WHATCHANNELISITON  REV
ABRIDGEDDICTIONARY
ISSO  REPEAT  MEAN
SWAMI  BANES  ASSESSED
TAN  OPCIT  SKAT  ETUI
RUG  NOUS  CABLENETWORK
USES  LTCALLEY  TAU  ROE
MALADY  UTICA  KAMBA
SUSPENSIONOFDISBELIEF
SLEET  GHOUL  ADELLE
QBS  IST  STOODOUT  ELLA
TAKESITSTOLL  TAHR  SAS
IBID  ALTS  MORSE  ART
PARDONER  PAGAN  SQYDS
REID  EARMEN  OAHU
PEDESTRIANAPPROACH
IDO  JUSTCANTGETOVERIT
FOR  ORSO  MOLES  NERUDA
SAT  BOSS  FEST  SEXED
```

45 Tearfully Yours

```
AZTEC  MOLTO  CRAM  NEBS
SUEDE  ILIAC  HERE  ALIE
IMMOVINGTOTHEBIGAPPLE
SAP  ILKA  OURS  REALM
OCS  REPLY  CAD  STE
THECHANGEWILLDOMEGOOD
HARTE  EASE  ALONE
ANNE  VAPO  PETRI  TOME
IGOTHIREDBYTHENYTIMES
SAVES  ERNES  ARTIST
RAM  SIR  AGREE  THU  TAD
ATASTE  ALOHA  BOOED
YOUCANTBEFUNNYFOREVER
EMIR  REEFS  ERIS  LEVO
AFOUL  PROV  STEER
ILLMISSEVERYONEDEARLY
MOA  ROT  ITEMS  ETS
LANGE  ASAP  OUST  THO
INCIDENTALLYAPRILFOOL
KEEN  GONG  OASIS  EAGLE
ERRS  OBOE  TYPEA  DRAMS
```

46 Terms of Engagement

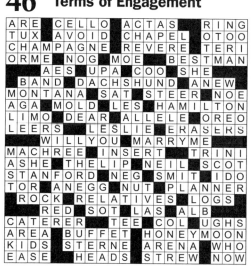

```
ARE  CELLO  ACTAS  RING
TUX  AVOID  CHAPEL  OTOO
CHAMPAGNE  REVERE  TERI
ORME  NOG  MOE  BESTMAN
AES  UPA  COO  SHE
BAND  DACHSHUND  ANEW
MONTANA  SAT  STEER  NOE
AGA  MOLD  LES  HAMILTON
LIMO  DEAR  ALLELE  OREO
LEERS  LESLIE  ERASERS
WILLYOU  MARRYME
MACHREE  INSERT  TRINI
ASHE  THELIP  NEIL  SCOT
STANFORD  NEG  SMIT  IDO
TOR  ANEGG  NUT  PLANNER
ROCK  RELATIVES  LOGS
RED  SOT  LAS  ALB
CATERER  TEE  COL  UGHS
AREA  BUFFET  HONEYMOON
KIDS  STERNE  ARENA  WHO
EASE  HEADS  STREW  NOW
```

47 Happy Birthday to Me

THE ARTIST / FORMERLY KNOWN AS PRINCE solved everything — the first two words total nine letters, matching TAMERLANE; the next four words total 21 letters, matching FETZER EAGLE PEAK MERLOT (which, amazingly, contains my first name *and* my last name), and FORMERLY, my unmatched 8-letter answer, no longer needed a match because it became part of the upper 21.

48 Connecting Flights

The cities forming the rectangle are highlighted in circles. They are, starting from the E in "Sam Waterston" and moving counterclockwise, EL PASO, OAKLAND, DALLAS, and SEATTLE. In addition, the four long theme answers all have the initials SW, so the airline had to be Southwest, which has daily flights to each of the four hidden cities.

49 At the Stamp Celebration

50 Simply Simpsons

Most Sunday crosswords are 21 squares on a side, and the fact that the distinctive closing notes of the "Simpsons" theme turned out to be exactly 21 notes was a huge stroke of luck. The other lucky breaks were 1) that the melody, if played in F major, has only black note (on a piano) and it's E FLAT, which, where it occurs in the grid, happens to fit perfectly snug against the edge, 2) the only way that "Maggie" could be hidable in anything is if there were something called an "aggie" that happened to follow something ending in M, and fortunately, the Aggies play at Texas A&M, 3) Homer Simpson's name happens to divide up into "Homer's imp son," which is a perfect clue for BART, and 4) the clue at 127 Across, which is where the music notes begin (on an F), opens with the words "Just so you know," which is a hint to the clue's actual three-letter answer, "FYI."

Do You Have "Puzzling" Friends or Relatives?
Give the Gift that Keeps Them That Way!

ORDER FORM
(*** PLEASE PRINT CLEARLY ***)

Your Name _____

Address _____

City/State/Zip _____

Phone (optional) (   ) _____ - _____

Recipient (if a gift) _____

Address _____

City/State/Zip _____

(Other recipients may be listed on the back.)

		Quantity	Subtotal
Best of Merl, Book 2	$14		
Best of Merl, Book 1	$14		
Merl Reagle's 100th Anniv. Puzzle Book	$14		
Merl Reagle's Sunday Crosswords	Vol. 18	$12		
	Vol. 17	$12		
	Vol. 16	$12		
	Vol. 15	$12		
	Vol. 14	$12		
	Vol. 12	$12		
	Vol. 11	$12		
	Vol. 10	$12		
	Vol. 9	$12		
	Vol. 8	$12		
	Vol. 4	$12		
	Vol. 3	$12		
	Vol. 2	$12		
	Vol. 1	$12		

FINAL TOTAL $_____

Send check or money order (payable to "The PuzzleWorks") to:
CROSSWORDS, P.O. BOX 15066, TAMPA FL 33684-5066.

ORDER FORM
(*** PLEASE PRINT CLEARLY ***)

Your Name _____

Address _____

City/State/Zip _____

Phone (optional) (   ) _____ - _____

Recipient (if a gift) _____

Address _____

City/State/Zip _____

(Other recipients may be listed on the back.)

		Quantity	Subtotal
Best of Merl, Book 2	$14		
Best of Merl, Book 1	$14		
Merl Reagle's 100th Anniv. Puzzle Book	$14		
Merl Reagle's Sunday Crosswords	Vol. 18	$12		
	Vol. 17	$12		
	Vol. 16	$12		
	Vol. 15	$12		
	Vol. 14	$12		
	Vol. 12	$12		
	Vol. 11	$12		
	Vol. 10	$12		
	Vol. 9	$12		
	Vol. 8	$12		
	Vol. 4	$12		
	Vol. 3	$12		
	Vol. 2	$12		
	Vol. 1	$12		

FINAL TOTAL $_____

Send check or money order (payable to "The PuzzleWorks") to:
CROSSWORDS, P.O. BOX 15066, TAMPA FL 33684-5066.

Send all correspondence and orders to:

The PuzzleWorks
P.O. Box 15066
Tampa FL 33684-5066

Or visit our website at www.sundaycrosswords.com